Reading Bitcoin
A Framework for Interpretation

Richard Rosdal

December 2025

This book is for informational and educational purposes only. It does not constitute financial, legal, investment, or tax advice. The views expressed are those of the author alone and are based on publicly available information, personal analysis, and interpretation at the time of writing. Markets, laws, and conditions may change.

Bitcoin and other digital assets involve risk, including the potential loss of capital. Readers should conduct their own research and consult qualified professionals before making financial decisions.

Written and finalized in December 2025.

First edition.

Printed in the United States of America.

Dedication

Here's a wish for health, wealth, and happiness.

For Jacob, Jared, Megan, Aaron, Emily, Elijah, and Emmanuel.

Acknowledgements

No book like this is written in isolation.

While the conclusions in these pages are my own, the thinking behind them was shaped over years by voices that challenged assumptions, clarified ideas, and forced deeper reasoning. Some did so through direct teaching, others through public analysis, debate, or example. All contributed meaningfully to how I came to understand Bitcoin—not as a trade, but as a structure.

Primary Influences

First, Michael Saylor deserves acknowledgement.

More than any other public figure, Saylor articulated Bitcoin not as a speculative asset, but as property, collateral, and permanent capital. His clarity around scarcity, time preference, and balance-sheet strategy helped move the conversation beyond price and toward structure. Whether one agrees with every expression or not, his influence on how institutions now think about Bitcoin is undeniable.

I am also grateful to Anthony Pompliano, whose work helped bridge Bitcoin from the technical into the practical, making complex ideas accessible without diluting their substance, and to Jordi Visser, whose macro perspective consistently challenged conventional financial frameworks and illuminated where Bitcoin fits within larger systemic transitions.

Thanks as well to Samson Mow, for his relentless focus on supply dynamics and game theory; Raoul Pal, for helping frame Bitcoin within global liquidity cycles; Tom Lee, for his data-driven approach to adoption and market structure; and Mark Moss, whose educational work has helped countless people understand monetary history and why Bitcoin represents a break from it.

I would also like to acknowledge Lyn Alden, for disciplined, systems-level macro analysis that prioritizes structure over narrative; Crypto Nutshell, for concise, accessible explanations that make complex Bitcoin concepts understandable without distortion; Simply Bitcoin, for consistent, signal-focused coverage that centers Bitcoin as a monetary system rather than a speculative trade; Swan Bitcoin, for advancing clear, education-first communication around Bitcoin custody, long-term holding, and financial responsibility; and British HODL, for principled advocacy that emphasizes sound money, sovereignty, and long-term thinking over short-term market narratives.

I also want to recognize Tim Warren and Taylor Shrum of *Investing Broz* (now *The Tim Warren Channel*). Their clear, disciplined approach to Bitcoin market structure, risk management, long-term thinking and technical analysis provided practical grounding during periods of volatility and noise, reinforcing patience over reaction.

Special thanks to Roy Balfour de Stadler for his careful reading of the manuscript and thoughtful feedback during the final stages of this project. His perspective helped sharpen several ideas and strengthened the clarity of the work.

Community & Ecosystem Acknowledgements

I am equally indebted to the broader Bitcoin community—analysts, builders, educators, and independent thinkers—whose conversations across platforms, podcasts, and conference stages continually refined my understanding. The more one studies any complex system, the clearer it becomes how much there still is to learn.

And finally, I acknowledge **Satoshi Nakamoto**.

Not as a personality, ideology, or figure to be interpreted—but as the creator of a system whose design choices (fixed supply, open participation, and no central issuer) made it durable without ongoing stewardship. By stepping away, the protocol was left to its rules and its users, which is the point of a permissionless monetary network.

How This Book Is Meant to Be Used

Written in December 2025, this work sits inside a moment of transition.

Bitcoin has already passed through multiple cycles of violent volatility, long stretches of compression, and repeated claims of failure. It has been declared finished more than once. It is still here.

What has changed is not sentiment, but posture.

Institutions are no longer observing from a distance.
Governments are no longer pretending Bitcoin can be ignored.
Rules are beginning to form around digital assets and digital credit.

Prices matter.
Liquidity matters.
Structure matters.

That timing is intentional.

What follows is written from inside the moment—as the system stands now, before its full shape is clear to everyone else.

For years, the central question surrounding Bitcoin was simple: would it fail outright?.

That question still exists—but it is no longer the only one.

Today, the conversation is broader: some still doubt durability, while others debate valuation, policy, and how Bitcoin fits into credit and balance sheets. That mix of views is healthy—and it's exactly why a testable framework matters.

This book does not argue that Bitcoin must succeed.
It does not predict price, timing, or adoption outcomes.
And it does not assume that current conditions will persist indefinitely.

What it offers is a framework for observing how systems behave when scarcity, credit, and liquidity interact under constraint.

If the conditions described here reverse—if sellable supply meaningfully returns, if liquidation replaces collateralization, or if an alternative system emerges with superior properties—the framework should fail visibly.

That is intentional.

The value of this book is not in being right. It is in being testable.

This book is not meant to be read only once.
And it is not meant to be read only now. It is meant to be used.

Some readers will be encountering Bitcoin for the first time—trying to understand why it persists, why it resists simple classification, and why it behaves differently from traditional assets.

Others will already hold it—perhaps for years—and are looking for a framework that explains why holding feels less speculative over time, even when volatility remains.

Some will approach this from institutions, policy, credit, or capital allocation—interested not in price targets, but in how systems adapt when scarcity cannot be expanded or negotiated.

Others will remain skeptical.

All of those perspectives belong here.

Read this book during a bull market, when confidence is high and mistakes come easily.
Return to it during uncertainty, when explanations multiply and clarity thins.
Come back to it years from now and ask a simple question:

Did this framework hold?

That question is welcome here.

This book is not about predicting prices or timelines.
It offers a way of seeing.

It focuses on constraints, not stories.
Incentives, not personalities.
Structure, not slogans.

When selling becomes less rational, it does not mean selling
disappears—it means it no longer functions as the system's
primary release mechanism.

Markets change.
Policies shift.
Technologies evolve.

But once a system reaches scale, certain pressures do not vanish.
They clarify.

Nothing here should be read as a forecast or an assertion of
inevitability. It examines how systems behave if certain conditions
persist—and how those behaviors change when they do not.

Think of this book as a map drawn mid-journey. It shows the
terrain as it looks now. Its value lies in whether it helps you keep
your bearings as the landscape continues to shift.

Read it closely.
Put it down.
Come back to it.

Agree where it holds.
Question it where it doesn't.

That is how this book is meant to live.

Foundational Terms

This section defines key terms as they are used **specifically in this book.**
They are not meant to be exhaustive, academic, or debated. They exist to ensure clarity, consistency, and shared footing before the analysis begins.

Readers already familiar with Bitcoin may skim this section. Readers new to the subject are encouraged to return to it as needed.

Bitcoin (BTC)

A decentralized digital asset governed by fixed rules, a permanently capped supply of 21 million units, and a global, permissionless network. In this book, Bitcoin is treated not as currency in motion, but as a **scarce reserve asset and collateral base**.

Satoshi (sat)

The smallest unit of Bitcoin. One Bitcoin equals 100 million Satoshis. This divisibility allows Bitcoin to function at both global settlement scale and granular accounting scale.

Scarcity

The condition in which supply cannot be increased in response to demand. Bitcoin's scarcity is enforced by code, not policy, and cannot be altered by discretion or authority.

Circulating Supply

Bitcoin that is actively available for trading or transfer. Coins held in long-term custody, cold storage, treasury reserves, or collateral arrangements are considered **effectively removed** from circulation.

Liquidity

The ease with which capital can move or be accessed. In this book, liquidity refers not only to buying power, but to **exit liquidity**—the ability to sell and recycle capital back into the system.

Exit Liquidity

The availability of willing buyers when holders choose to sell. Bitcoin increasingly absorbs liquidity without reliably returning it, altering traditional market dynamics.

Collateral

An asset pledged to secure borrowing. Bitcoin's durability, scarcity, and resistance to dilution make it uniquely suited to function as **long-term collateral rather than consumable capital**.

Bitcoin-backed Lending

A financial arrangement that allows holders to access liquidity by borrowing against Bitcoin instead of selling it. This mechanism reduces forced selling and lengthens holding horizons.

Custody

The secure holding of Bitcoin, either personally (self-custody) or through regulated institutional providers. Custody structures influence whether Bitcoin remains liquid or becomes structurally illiquid.

Fiat Currency

Government-issued money used as a medium of exchange, unit of account, and tax rail. In this book, fiat is treated as functional for transactions, but unreliable as a long-term store of value.

Repricing

A process in which price adjusts sharply due to structural changes in supply and demand, rather than speculation or enthusiasm. Repricing replaces traditional cyclical resets once exit liquidity disappears.

Market Phase

A period defined by observable behavior rather than narrative or expectation. The term is used instead of "regime" to emphasize adaptability without implying control or permanence.

Generational Wealth

Assets held with no intended sale, designed to preserve purchasing power across decades rather than cycles. Bitcoin increasingly occupies this role.

These definitions are not conclusions.
They are the vocabulary required to understand what follows.

With terms aligned, the story can begin.

Chapter 5—Transitions, Not Verdicts 70

Chapter 6—Macro Is Pressure, Not Cause........................... 75

Chapter 7—Liquidity Without Exit 83

Introduction

Drafted: December 2025

This work reflects a long-form thinking process shaped by experience, disciplined curiosity, and the deliberate use of modern tools to sharpen—not replace—human judgment.

Most people encounter markets through headlines and charts. They react to what has already happened and try to project it forward. That approach works until it doesn't. Structural change rarely announces itself. It unfolds quietly, long before price responds.

Over the past few years, something fundamental has shifted beneath the surface of the financial system. Not a rally. Not a narrative. A change in structure.

Bitcoin is no longer behaving like a speculative asset searching for validation. It is increasingly treated as collateral—something held, locked, and modeled rather than traded. At the same time, the systems built around it—ETFs, corporate treasuries, balance sheets, and emerging policy frameworks—are absorbing supply faster than most observers appreciate.

This creates a familiar pattern in unfamiliar form.

When supply tightens structurally and demand is forced to operate within constraints, price does not move gradually. It reprices. And repricing is rarely linear, polite, or well-timed for consensus.

At its core, what this book describes is not a price cycle, but a power cycle.

Throughout this book, the word 'cycle' is used for familiarity—not because Bitcoin repeats mechanically, but because market language changes more slowly than market structure, and what follows behaves less like repetition and more like repricing under constraint.

Power in Bitcoin is defined by custody, balance sheets, access to liquidity, time horizon, and the ability—or inability—to sell. Across each cycle, power transfers quietly from weak hands to strong hands during periods of indifference and stress, then disperses back into the market during periods of confidence and excess.

Price is not the driver of this process. It is the output—often delayed, often violent, and frequently misunderstood.

This distinction matters because market participants are not playing the same game.

Swing traders operate on shorter time horizons. They seek volatility, momentum, and liquidity, accepting that precision and speed matter more than long-term conviction. For traders, certain phases of the cycle—particularly compression and early expansion—can offer structurally safer conditions, where liquidity is improving and trends are becoming defined.

Long-horizon investors operate differently. Their edge is not speed, but patience. Investors benefit most during accumulation and late-correction phases, when power is quietly transferring and narratives are weakest. For them, excessive trading during expansion often increases risk rather than reducing it.

This thesis is offered primarily from the investor's perspective. It does not dismiss trading, but places it in context. Understanding where you are in the cycle matters more than any individual trade. Often the more durable advantage is knowing when *not* to trade.

The metaphor used throughout this book is simple: firewood and matches.

Firewood represents conditions—the slow accumulation of prerequisites that make a system vulnerable to catch fire. Matches represent catalysts—often small, sometimes accidental, and frequently invisible until after the fact. Most people watch for flames. By then, the outcome is already determined.

The aim here is to document the firewood—and to explain how power moves through the cycle before price makes it obvious.

This book does not attempt to identify specific dates or events. It offers no guarantees. Instead, it lays out a way of identifying where power sits within the cycle—so expectations can be adjusted before narratives shift and hindsight takes over.

Along the way, the lens widens beyond Bitcoin itself. Energy systems, materials supply chains, and monetary confidence share a common trait: they cannot be rushed. Uranium, rare earths, silver, and digital scarcity rhyme in ways that become obvious only under stress.

This work is not meant to be read once. It is meant to be returned to—during accumulation, during expansion, and especially during correction—so the reader can recognize which phase of the cycle is unfolding and respond with clarity rather than emotion.

By the time everyone sees the move, the power has already shifted.

What This Book Is—and Is Not

This book does not argue inevitability.
It argues structural pressure under identifiable conditions.

The progression described is probabilistic, not deterministic.

This is not a forecast.

It does not attempt to time markets, call tops, or predict price targets.

It does not argue that Bitcoin will replace fiat, overthrow governments, or eliminate credit.

Instead, it describes how Bitcoin behaves once it becomes a long-duration store of value, permanent collateral rather than inventory, an asset that is increasingly held rather than traded, and a balance-sheet anchor rather than a speculative position.

These shifts are already visible. The book does not attempt to accelerate them or defend them. It simply maps their implications.

Pressure vs. Cause

One of the central distinctions in this book is between pressure and cause.

Macroeconomic events—rates, liquidity, currencies, and policy decisions—do not *create* Bitcoin's behavior. They apply pressure to structures that already exist. What breaks, or accelerates, was prepared long before the pressure arrived.

Confusing pressure with cause leads to reactive thinking and misplaced certainty. Understanding the difference allows for preparation rather than prediction.

How This Book Was Written

What follows is not a stream of opinions or a collection of predictions.

Each chapter began as a hypothesis, then was challenged, stress-tested, simplified, and rewritten until it could be expressed clearly without relying on jargon, authority, or persuasion. Ideas that did not hold up under repeated scrutiny were removed. Arguments that required excessive defense were discarded.

Throughout this process, I worked in collaboration with an artificial intelligence system—not as a source of conclusions, but as a tool for sharpening reasoning. The conclusions are mine. The responsibility for errors is mine. The method reflects a broader shift now underway: humans using machine intelligence not to replace thinking, but to refine it.

This matters because Bitcoin itself is a system that rewards clarity, structure, and discipline over narrative and impulse.

What Volatility Is Signaling

Bitcoin is often described as volatile. That description misses the point.

Volatility is not a flaw; it is a signal. It reflects a system adjusting to constraints that remain poorly understood by most participants. As those constraints harden through long-term holding, institutional custody, collateralization, and sovereign interest, the nature of volatility itself changes.

Cycles that once reset through selling and capitulation lose their force. Liquidity no longer guarantees exit. Price discovery becomes discontinuous rather than gradual.

This is not a dramatic break.
It is a quiet transition.

How to Read This Book

This book is structured like a building. Each chapter supports the next. Skipping ahead may still be interesting, but the logic is cumulative.

If you find yourself thinking, *"I've felt this, but never articulated it,"* then the book is doing its job.

A Note on Certainty

The analysis does not claim certainty about the future.
It claims clarity about structure.

Structure does not guarantee outcomes, but it does constrain them. Once those constraints are understood, many questions stop being interesting—and others become unavoidable.

Why This Was Written

Many people sense that something has changed in Bitcoin but lack the language to describe it.

The intent is for those less interested in being right than in seeing clearly.
Not to convince.
Not to persuade.
But to orient.

The focus here is not on whether Bitcoin will rise in price. It is an explanation of why, once certain structural conditions are met, selling stops making sense for a growing share of participants—and what happens to markets when that behavior becomes widespread.

Most financial analysis focuses on triggers: headlines, policies, announcements, and narratives. This book focuses on structure—on ownership, liquidity, and supply that does not reliably return once acquired.

Those forces work slowly, quietly, and often invisibly—until they don't.

The core claim of this book is simple: once Bitcoin is widely treated as long-term collateral rather than short-term inventory, markets stop clearing the way they used to. Selling becomes optional for some, impossible for others, and price begins to behave less like a cycle and more like a repricing event.

Everything that follows explains why that shift is already underway—and why it matters.

Chapter 1 begins with a simple observation: most Bitcoin mistakes are not made in fear—they are made in excitement.

Chapter 1—The Assumption

Drafted: December 2025

"Most of the time, the problem isn't that we don't know the answer.
It's that we don't question the assumption."
— Author Unknown

The World We Expected to Work

For most people, the rules were straightforward.

Work hard. Save what you can. Trust the system. Don't take reckless risks.

This wasn't foolish. It was reasonable. It was encouraged. And for a long time, it worked well enough that questioning it felt unnecessary.

Money was expected to hold its value.

Debt was expected to stay manageable.

Time was expected to help, not hurt.

These ideas weren't extreme. They were passed down. And beliefs that are inherited rarely get examined closely.

The Assumption No One Really Questioned

At the center of modern finance sat one quiet assumption:

Tomorrow will work the same way yesterday did.

That belief carried more weight than most people realized.

- It made rising debt feel normal.
- It made shrinking savings feel tolerable.
- It allowed trust to replace restraint.

As long as things kept working, there was little reason to stop and ask harder questions. For a while, that was enough.

What People Did Wrong (Which Was Very Little)

Most people didn't behave irresponsibly. They saved where they were told it was safe. They diversified the way professionals advised. They trusted that decisions were being made with long-term stability in mind.

In short, they followed the rules.

The discomfort many people feel today isn't the result of bad choices. It's the result of reasonable choices made inside a system that slowly changed its own assumptions.

That difference matters.

When Stability Became a Performance

Over time, looking stable became more important than being stable.

Growth slowed, but borrowing increased.

Productivity lagged, but liquidity expanded.

Warning signs faded, but confidence stayed high. This wasn't driven by bad intentions—it was driven by convenience.

Maintaining confidence is easier than enforcing restraint—especially when the consequences don't show up right away.

Why Systems Don't Break Gradually

We often talk about financial systems as if they adjust smoothly, but they don't.

They absorb pressure quietly for long periods—and then they change all at once.

Most structural problems stay out of sight until they can't be ignored. By the time they become obvious, the chance to prepare has usually passed.

That's not unusual. It's how these things tend to work.

When Systems Stop Moving Together

For a long time, certain things were expected to rise together.

If productivity increased, wages would follow. If markets grew, opportunity would spread. If technology improved efficiency, life would gradually feel easier.

That relationship was the glue that made the system feel coherent.

What happens when it breaks is harder to notice at first.

Financial markets can continue rising while daily life becomes more constrained. Economic output can improve even as purchasing power erodes. Innovation can accelerate while stability feels harder to maintain.

The numbers still reconcile on paper—but they no longer reconcile in lived experience.

Divergence isn't a crisis. It's a separation. It's the moment when systems that once moved together quietly begin to drift apart. Growth continues, but it concentrates. Progress remains visible, but it stops feeling shared.

When divergence takes hold, the system doesn't feel broken—it feels confusing. Effort produces less return. Saving feels less rewarding. Time, which once helped, begins to work against you.

People sense this long before they can explain it. And they often assume the problem is personal. It usually isn't.

One reason divergence is so hard to see is that it often hides inside things that feel stable for a long time.

In the decades after World War II, suburban housing often felt easy and predictable. Prices moved steadily, listings appeared regularly, and most buyers assumed that if they missed one house, another would come along. At the same time, something very different was happening underneath. Buildable land near growing cities was steadily used up, zoning rules hardened, and neighborhoods quietly filled in. Buyers still felt like they had options, even as the system tightened underneath. That divergence went largely unnoticed because nothing felt tight yet. When demand eventually rose, prices didn't adjust gradually—they jumped, revealing that the constraint had already formed long before it became visible.

Why This Moment Feels Different

Many people sense that something has shifted, even if they can't quite explain it.

Effort doesn't seem to go as far as it used to. Saving feels riskier than it should. Time no longer feels like an ally. This isn't pessimism— it's paying attention.

Systems don't announce when they're reaching their limits.

They show it through behavior—often while insisting everything is fine.

The Arrival of an Unintended Alternative

Bitcoin didn't show up with a plan to fix everything.

It wasn't created to save the financial system. It wasn't meant to replace institutions. It wasn't expected to matter beyond a small group of enthusiasts.

For years, ignoring it was easy. Then something unexpected happened.

Bitcoin didn't ask for trust. It didn't respond to policy changes. It didn't adjust itself to fit expectations. It just kept operating the same way.

In a world built around constant adjustment, that difference turned out to matter.

Why This Book Isn't About Price

This book isn't about getting rich.

It isn't about trading tactics, predicting short-term moves, or chasing price targets.

It's about understanding a system—and what happens when an alternative exists that doesn't depend on the same assumptions as everything else.

This book isn't asking you to believe anything.

It's asking you to notice something.

Assumptions matter most when we don't question them. And when one breaks, the effects aren't always immediate—but they are permanent.

The chapters ahead explore how those assumptions formed, why they went unchallenged for so long, and what happens when a flexible system encounters something designed not to bend.

Not as a revolution—as a reorientation.

Chapter 2—The Failure

Drafted: December 2025

"In the end, we do not merely discover that the old maps are
wrong.
We discover that the landscape itself has changed beneath our
feet."
— Anonymous

The modern financial system did not fail because of greed.
It did not fail because of corruption.
And it did not fail because people stopped believing in it.

It failed because its assumptions stopped matching reality.

For decades, the system functioned well enough that its internal
tensions remained hidden. Growth masked fragility. Liquidity
softened leverage. Confidence substituted for discipline. The
system appeared to work not because it was sound, but because
pressure had not yet tested its limits.

That period has now passed.

The failure we are living through is not sudden, and it is not
dramatic in the way collapse is often imagined. There is no
single moment when everything breaks. Instead, the failure
expresses itself as ongoing instability—a system that must be
repeatedly rescued, adjusted, explained, and defended in order
to keep operating.

This is not a political claim.
It is an engineering one.

A System Built on Assumptions

Every financial system rests on assumptions. Most remain invisible, like gravity to someone walking down the street. You do not need to understand them for the system to function—until those assumptions stop holding.

At its core, the modern monetary system assumed that:

- Debt could expand faster than obligations came due
- Trust could be manufactured through policy
- Risk could be modeled, managed, and redistributed indefinitely
- Central coordination could outperform decentralized discipline
- Future growth would justify present borrowing

For a time, these assumptions appeared to hold. Productivity rose. Markets deepened. Credit expanded. Living standards improved. The system delivered results, and success reinforced belief.

But assumptions rarely fail all at once. They erode gradually, then structurally, and finally irreversibly.

The system is not fragile because participants are reckless. It is fragile because its assumptions only hold under conditions of stability.

Those assumptions are seldom stated outright. They do not need to be. They are reinforced through habit, repetition, and long periods in which nothing appears to break.

Money is assumed to retain purchasing power over time.
Saving is assumed to be rewarded, not penalized.
Debt is assumed to remain serviceable as long as growth continues.

Institutions are assumed to manage risk competently enough to justify trust.

These beliefs feel reasonable—until the conditions that support them fade.

What makes them dangerous is that they are conditional. They depend on steady growth, predictable policy, and contained volatility. When those conditions persist, the system feels robust. When they weaken, the assumptions do not adjust smoothly.

They fail together.

How Failure Actually Appears

This is why financial breakdowns often feel sudden. The system does not weaken in public. It weakens in private, accumulating strain beneath the surface while behavior continues as if the old rules still apply.

People do not stop believing in the system because it becomes inefficient. They stop trusting it when it no longer behaves the way it promised to.

That loss of confidence is not emotional.
It is observational.

At first, the response is subtle. Saving feels less effective. Holding cash feels riskier. Waiting begins to feel like a cost rather than a virtue. People adjust not because they have a theory, but because incentives change.

Those adjustments compound.

As more participants act defensively, the system becomes increasingly dependent on intervention to preserve normalcy.

Liquidity must be injected. Rates must be managed. Volatility must be smoothed. Each intervention buys time, but each also increases reliance on the next one.

Over time, the system stops correcting itself. Stability is no longer produced organically. It is administered.

This is not collapse.
It is saturation.

The Point of Saturation

The failure did not begin with excess. It began with saturation.

Debt reached a scale where it no longer funded expansion, but merely sustained existing obligations. New borrowing stopped creating new capacity and instead served to roll forward the past. Policy responses grew larger, not because ambition increased, but because effectiveness declined.

This is the hallmark of a system operating beyond its optimal range.

At this stage, every solution produces a secondary cost:

- Lower rates inflate asset prices while eroding savings
- Higher rates stabilize currency while stressing debt
- Liquidity supports markets while distorting price signals
- Austerity restores balance while fracturing social cohesion

There is no clean path forward—only trade-offs.

Signal Breakdown

As strain accumulated, another failure emerged: signals stopped working.

Prices no longer reflected risk.
Rates no longer reflected time preference.
Markets no longer cleared—they were managed.

When intervention becomes persistent, information degrades. Participants lose the ability to distinguish strength from support, demand from subsidy, or value from momentum. Decision-making shifts from analysis toward anticipation of response.

This is not a conspiracy.
It is an inevitable outcome of continuous control.

The system did not lose credibility because people lost faith.
It lost credibility because it lost reliable feedback.

The Confidence Trap

Confidence is often mistaken for stability.
It is not.

Confidence is belief in stability.

A system can remain confident long after it has become fragile—especially when alternatives are limited. Participation continues not because the system works well, but because exiting feels riskier than remaining inside it.

This creates a trap.

As fragility increases, confidence must be defended more aggressively—through messaging, guarantees, and emergency measures. Over time, preserving belief becomes more important than restoring structure.

At that point, the system is no longer adaptive.
It is defensive.

Why This Failure Is Different

Financial failures are often cyclical. Recessions reduce excess. Defaults restore balance. Risk is repriced and growth resumes.

This failure is different because the mechanisms that once corrected the system are now constrained by the system itself.

Defaults are politically difficult.
Market clearing is destabilizing.
Discipline is recessionary.

The system cannot fully correct without threatening its own continuity.

That is not collapse—but it is lock-in.

The Space a Failure Creates

Every structural failure creates space.

- Not for rebellion
- Not for ideology
- But for adaptation

When a system can no longer perform its original functions—preserving value across time, coordinating trust, pricing risk—alternatives do not emerge because people demand them. They emerge because the system requires relief from its own constraints.

This is not a moral moment.
It is a mechanical one.

The failure does not ask what people believe.
It asks what still works.

From Failure to Response

The failure did not announce itself with a crash. It revealed itself through persistent intervention, distorted signals, and shrinking margins of control.

Once that failure exists, the question is no longer whether something new *should* appear.

The question becomes:

What kind of response fits a world where the old assumptions no longer hold?

That response is the subject of the next chapter.

Chapter 3—The Response

Drafted: December 2025

"A purely peer-to-peer version of electronic cash would allow online payments to be sent directly from one party to another without going through a financial institution."
— Satoshi Nakamoto, Bitcoin White Paper (2008)

When people begin to doubt that money will do what they expect it to do, behavior changes.

Not because people become irrational, but because survival demands adjustment. Saving feels unsafe. Waiting feels costly. Standing still begins to feel like risk.

Those adjustments don't happen randomly.

This chapter explains what that response looks like over time.

When Alternatives Appear

When systems fail, alternatives don't arrive with announcements. They emerge quietly, often dismissed at first, and only become visible in hindsight.

They don't ask to be believed.

They don't try to persuade.

They simply exist—and allow people to opt in.

One such response appeared at the edges of the financial system during the last major crisis.

Where Bitcoin Came From

In 2008, as confidence in the global financial system was breaking down, a pseudonymous developer using the name Satoshi Nakamoto published a short paper describing a new kind of money.

The system was called Bitcoin.

It wasn't designed to fix the existing system. It didn't rely on trust, policy, or discretion. It simply removed the assumption that money would be managed well.

Bitcoin didn't emerge to chase price movements. It emerged from skepticism about whether existing systems could reliably be trusted.

The software was released quietly in 2009. It was open-source, functional, and unremarkable in appearance. There was no company behind it, no marketing, and no promise that it would be worth anything.

The network grew because people chose to run the code, verify transactions, and accept the system's rules. Bitcoin did not become valuable by declaration. It functioned consistently, without permission, and without requiring trust.

Eventually, that reliability began to matter.

Bitcoin moved beyond experimentation and began to be exchanged and held because others were willing to use it.

Structure and Scale

Bitcoin's structure was deliberately simple.

The total supply was fixed at 21 million coins permanently. Each coin was divisible into 100 million units, later called satoshis (sats)—allowing the system to function at any scale, from small payments to global settlement.

At the time, this structure seemed theoretical. There was no price to optimize for, no adoption curve to model, and no expectation that all units would ever matter.

That uncertainty shaped how Bitcoin was first used.

The First "Known" Transaction

In 2010, a developer named Laszlo Hanyecz traded 10,000 Bitcoin for two pizzas.

At the time, this wasn't seen as wasteful or symbolic. It was practical. Bitcoin had no established value, and the transaction proved something more important than price: that the system worked.

The pizzas weren't expensive. The bitcoins weren't precious.

What mattered was that a digital unit, governed by fixed rules and no central authority, had been exchanged for something real.

Only later did the scale become obvious.

A Slice of Perspective

The famous Bitcoin pizza story is usually told as a joke.

Someone spent 10,000 Bitcoin on two pizzas.

At today's price, those pizzas would cost hundreds of millions of dollars.

That framing misses the point.

The lesson isn't that buying pizza was a mistake.
The lesson is that Bitcoin was being used as currency, before
anyone understood it would become a reserve asset.

At the time, Bitcoin was treated like cash.
Cash is for lunch.

But as time passed, something changed. Bitcoin didn't just
move in price—it began to hold purchasing power across time.
And when that happens, behavior changes.

People stop asking, "What can I buy with this?"
They start asking, "Why would I spend it?"

Now take the same idea forward.

Buying burgers with Bitcoin today doesn't feel strange.
Over time, it will.

Not because burgers change—
but because Bitcoin does.

No one buys groceries with gold.
No one pays rent with treasury reserves.

They could—they just don't.

That's not ideology.
That's instinct.

From Experiment to Ecosystem

What makes Bitcoin relevant today is not that it appeared during
a crisis, but that it persisted long after the crisis passed.

It continued through recoveries, expansions, policy shifts, bubbles, crashes, bans, dismissals, and indifference. In the process, the network grew—quietly—into the largest distributed system of its kind, maintained not by mandate but by voluntary participation.

Code became a network as people began running nodes and verifying transactions. Over time, participation expanded—first miners, then developers, and then long-term holders. An ecosystem formed without a central authority coordinating it.

By the time most people began paying attention, Bitcoin had already survived long enough, and grown large enough, to matter.

Resistance and Tension

This growth did not go uncontested. From the beginning, Bitcoin faced resistance from the existing financial system— institutions, regulators, intermediaries, and structures whose authority depended on money remaining permissioned, mutable, and centrally managed.

What Bitcoin introduced was a system that operated without discretion or gatekeepers—once deployed, it continued according to its rules.

The tension between these two approaches—one rooted in management and control, the other in rules and persistence—has shaped Bitcoin's evolution from the start and continues to shape how it behaves today.

Why Cycles Appear

Once Bitcoin reached scale, behavior around it stopped being theoretical.

- Some people accumulated it.
- Others traded it.
- Some leveraged it.
- Some were forced to sell it.

Those behaviors did not occur in isolation. They interacted—repeatedly—creating recognizable phases over time.

These phases are not unique to Bitcoin. They appear wherever a scarce asset meets unequal access to capital, differing time horizons, and human emotion.

Bitcoin simply makes them easier to see.

The next chapter begins where this cycle starts—not with headlines or price moves, but with accumulation and supply.

Before anything looks obvious, power is already moving—quietly.

Chapter 4—Supply Is Destiny

Drafted: December 2025

"In the short run, the market is a voting machine. In the long run, it is a weighing machine."
— Benjamin Graham

The previous chapter described what happens when Bitcoin reaches scale.

It showed how a fixed-supply system, once large enough to matter, produces recurring phases—accumulation, compression, ignition, expansion, and correction—driven by unequal access to capital, differing time horizons, and human behavior.

That chapter established the pattern.

This chapter examines the constraint beneath it.

Because those phases do not emerge from sentiment or narrative alone. They arise from a more basic condition: how much Bitcoin is available to be sold at each stage of the cycle—and how that availability changes over time.

Accumulation, compression, and correction are not abstract concepts. They are expressions of supply moving—quietly— from one set of hands to another.

To understand why these phases unfold in this order, and why the most important shifts often occur when nothing appears to be happening, look beneath price and behavior to supply itself.

Not total supply—available supply.

That is the focus of this chapter.

Every market talks about demand.
Few understand supply.

Demand explains movement.
Supply explains why that movement can become extreme.

Over time, Bitcoin's defining characteristic becomes constraint—not theoretical constraint, but the practical question of how much is available to sell.

This chapter explains why supply, not demand, determines the shape and severity of Bitcoin's cycle.

Why Supply Matters More Than Demand

Demand is loud.
Supply is quiet.

Demand announces itself through price, headlines, and attention. Supply works invisibly, shaping outcomes long before they appear obvious.

In most markets, supply responds to price. Higher prices bring more production. Lower prices reduce it. Bitcoin breaks this feedback loop entirely. Its supply does not respond to demand, price, policy, or optimism.

That alone changes how markets behave under stress.

But the more important distinction is this:

Total supply is not the same as available supply.

Bitcoin's fixed cap is widely understood. What is rarely understood is how much Bitcoin is for sale.

Markets move not when demand increases, but when demand meets insufficient supply.

That is not a refutation of supply mechanics. It is the real world asserting that constraints meet incentives on both sides.

When those branches dominate, scarcity does not vanish—but repricing can stall, reverse, or take longer than expected.

• Demand can be redirected (a superior reserve asset or protocol emerges).

• Demand can be priced out temporarily (credit tightening, recession, risk-off correlation).

• Demand can be suppressed (policy, custody restrictions, capital controls).

• Demand can plateau (fatigue, saturation, better alternatives).

To keep this framework honest, we should name the demand-side branches that can interrupt the supply story:

Demand still matters—especially the kind that disappears when conditions change.

In other words: tightening liquid supply can magnify price movement, but it does not guarantee it.

It is a constraint.

Supply is not a prophecy.

Liquid Supply vs. Total Supply

Bitcoin's total supply is capped.
Its liquid supply is variable—and shrinking.

Liquid supply consists of Bitcoin held by participants who:

- are willing to sell
- must sell
- or are structurally exposed to selling

As Bitcoin matures, more of its supply migrates into forms that are:

- long-duration
- institutionally custodied
- balance-sheet protected
- or collateralized rather than liquidated

When Bitcoin leaves circulation, it does not announce itself.
It simply stops responding to price signals.

This is what creates compression.

The Institutional Power Stack

Supply does not disappear randomly.
It is absorbed systematically.

This is not a coordinated structure. It emerges organically as different participants respond to the same constraint.

The modern Bitcoin cycle is defined by what can best be described as an institutional power stack—a layered system that captures supply and extends holding horizons.

Each layer reduces the probability that Bitcoin returns to market during stress.

Before examining that stack, it helps to understand where Bitcoin can actually sit—and why that matters.

Where Bitcoin Can Be Held

Bitcoin is not stored in one place.

It exists on a global ledger, but access to it—and the behavior it enables—depends entirely on how and where it is held.

Broadly, Bitcoin tends to sit in four types of places, each with very different implications for supply.

Personal Wallets

A personal wallet is software or hardware that allows an individual to control their own private keys.

Private keys are the cryptographic credentials that prove ownership and allow Bitcoin to be moved.

Bitcoin held this way is:

- controlled directly by the owner
- stored outside of any company or institution
- accessible without relying on another party's permission

To sell Bitcoin held in a personal wallet, the owner typically transfers it to an exchange or sells it directly to another person.

Personal wallets are designed for secure storage, not frequent movement.

They prioritize safety, control, and long-term holding over speed or convenience.

This form of ownership offers maximum control, but places responsibility for security and access entirely on the individual.

Exchanges

Exchanges are companies that allow people to buy and sell Bitcoin.

Bitcoin held on an exchange is:

- already in a trading environment
- easy to buy or sell quickly
- influenced by market activity and sentiment

Because exchanges hold Bitcoin on behalf of many users, the owner does not directly control the private keys while funds remain on the platform.

Exchanges are designed for movement, not long-term storage.

They prioritize access, speed, and liquidity—not permanence.

For this reason, many long-term holders use exchanges primarily as on-ramps and off-ramps, moving Bitcoin into personal wallets or custody solutions once transactions are complete.

From a supply perspective, Bitcoin held on exchanges is the most immediately responsive to price.

Regulated Custody

Regulated custodians are licensed financial entities that hold Bitcoin on behalf of clients.

These are typically:

- banks or trust companies
- custodians used by investment funds and retirement accounts
- entities subject to financial regulation and oversight

Bitcoin held this way:

- is governed by rules and procedures
- is not moved casually
- is often held for long periods

This structure is required for institutions and investment products like ETFs.

Bitcoin held in regulated custody behaves less like trading inventory and more like a long-duration asset.

Collateralized or Structured Holdings

Some Bitcoin is held not for sale, but for use—pledged to support loans or financial arrangements.

In these cases:

- Bitcoin is posted as collateral
- liquidity is accessed through borrowing
- selling is avoided unless required

Bitcoin held in this way is functionally removed from day-to-day market activity, even though ownership remains unchanged.

Bitcoin as a Sovereign Balance-Sheet Asset

This section establishes the conceptual framework. The market implications of sovereign adoption are addressed later.

Bitcoin does not replace fiat money, Treasury markets, or fiscal discipline. It interacts with them differently.

A more accurate way to think about Bitcoin is as a **balance-sheet asset**, not as a currency meant to be spent.

If a sovereign were to build a meaningful Bitcoin reserve, Bitcoin would not be used to pay down national debt. It would be used the same way durable assets are used everywhere else: **as collateral**.

The idea is simple:

- hold a scarce, durable asset
- borrow conservatively against it
- avoid selling it
- refinance over time

Corporations already do this with equity.
Individuals do it with real estate.
Bitcoin-backed lending already exists on a smaller scale.

Applied carefully, a sovereign Bitcoin reserve could:

- sit alongside traditional reserves
- help refinance a portion of outstanding debt
- reduce pressure to monetize at the margins
- add long-term balance-sheet flexibility

Bitcoin as a Reserve Asset, Not a Transactional Currency

Bitcoin behaves less like a transactional currency and more like a reserve asset.

Reserve assets are not consumed.
They are collateralized.

Seen through that lens, borrowing against Bitcoin reflects a familiar pattern: when an asset proves durable across time, participants prefer to access liquidity without selling it.

Selling the asset to fund consumption misunderstands its function. A reserve exists to support activity without being consumed by it—much like valuable artwork is preserved while economic value is built around it. The distinction is not moral or ideological. It is structural.

Bitcoin's utility does not emerge from frequent spending.
It emerges from how it behaves when held—how often it is sold, how often it is borrowed against, and how long it remains dormant.

Long-term holding increases scarcity and reduces speculative churn. When Bitcoin is held or collateralized rather than spent, it tends to move less frequently—reducing exposure to operational risk over time. Fewer transactions mean fewer exposed keys, fewer operational failures, and fewer opportunities for loss.

Time Horizons Are Power

Power in Bitcoin is not measured by conviction.
It is measured by time.

Holders with:

- short time horizons
- leverage
- or liquidity constraints

are forced to act.

Holders with:

- long-duration balance sheets
- access to credit
- or institutional mandates

can wait.

As ownership shifts toward the latter, supply becomes increasingly insensitive to price declines. This does not eliminate corrections. It changes their character.

Why This Phase Feels Invisible

Supply-driven phases are boring by design.

Nothing appears to happen:

- price stalls
- narratives conflict
- volatility compresses
- Commentators grow impatient.
- Participants lose interest.

This is precisely when structural changes occur.

Firewood is not exciting.
It is necessary.

What to Watch Instead of Price

During supply-driven phases, price is the least informative signal.

More useful questions include:

- Is Bitcoin leaving liquid venues?
- Are holders selling—or borrowing?
- Is volatility compressing despite macro pressure?
- Are institutions accumulating quietly rather than announcing loudly?

These signals rarely trend on social media. They shape outcomes anyway.

Supply Can Tighten Even While Price Weakens

During compression, price can decline even as supply quietly tightens.

At various points in Bitcoin's history, exchange balances have continued to fall while price drifted lower—a divergence that confuses observers focused solely on charts. This pattern reflects accumulation, not abandonment.

The chart below illustrates Bitcoin exchange balances (blue) alongside price (white). Even as price weakened, supply continued to leave liquid venues, illustrating how accumulation can occur quietly beneath declining prices.

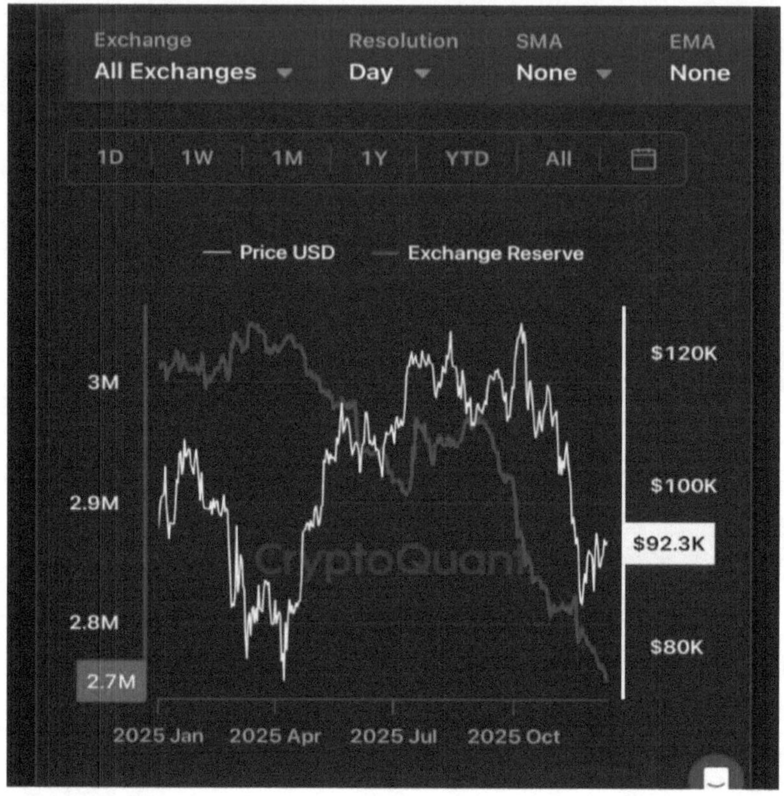

Exchange balance data shows a long-term decline in Bitcoin held on exchanges, consistent with tightening liquid supply.

The chart does not show who is buying. It shows the amount of Bitcoin that is no longer available. That distinction matters.

Supply Compression Is Necessary — Not Sufficient

Supply compression alone does not guarantee repricing.

A permanently tightening float creates structural pressure, but price requires both constraint and participation.

If global demand for Bitcoin were to plateau or decline — due to regulatory hostility, technological displacement, or capital preference shifts — supply inelasticity would not force repricing. It would instead produce stagnation.

This framework therefore rests on a conditional claim:

If demand remains structurally positive while supply becomes increasingly unavailable, repricing pressure accumulates.

If demand weakens materially, compression alone is insufficient.

Why Price Doesn't Reflect Accumulation

Large buyers rarely acquire Bitcoin through public exchanges.

Institutions, funds, and sovereign entities typically buy via Over-the-Counter (OTC) desks—private transactions negotiated off-exchange.

These purchases:

- do not lift visible market price
- do not consume public order books
- often result in Bitcoin moving directly into custody or long-term storage

From the market's perspective, nothing happens.

Price can drift lower due to marginal selling, while large quantities of Bitcoin are quietly removed from liquid venues and never offered back.

This is how exchange supply can fall even as price weakens.

OTC activity does not announce itself.
It removes supply without signaling demand.

When underlying supply forces start to matter more, price often lags what's changing.

Price can move without resolution.
Volatility can appear without redistribution.
Stress can emerge without delivering a clear signal.

These periods invite error.

Observers rush to assign meaning, declare failure, or treat ambiguity as evidence that something has broken. But markets do not always speak in conclusions. Sometimes they speak in tests.

And at the far end of the spectrum sits something like the Mona Lisa.

No one asks how many pizzas or burgers it can buy.
Those questions don't apply.

Its value isn't transactional.
It's custodial.

It exists to be held, protected, and passed forward—not circulated.

Bitcoin isn't art.

But it is moving along a similar curve.

As an asset proves it can preserve value across longer periods of time, it naturally moves out of circulation and into reserve. Spending stops not because people are greedy, but because it stops making sense.

That's the quiet transition most people miss.

Bitcoin didn't fail as money. It began to behave like something people stopped spending.

The Cycle, at a Glance

I'll use 'cycle' as familiarity, but these are better understood as Market Phases—behavioral patterns that repeat without fixed timing.

The Bitcoin power cycle consists of five recurring phases:

1. Accumulation
2. Compression
3. Ignition
4. Expansion
5. Correction

These phases do not operate on fixed timelines. They stretch, compress, overlap, and occasionally stall. What remains consistent is their order, not their duration. Each phase transfers power differently. They describe recurring behavioral patterns, not timing models.

Understanding the cycle is not about forecasting price. It's about understanding who gains control, when—and why.

Phase One: Accumulation—When No One Is Interested

Accumulation begins when confidence is low and attention has moved elsewhere. Price is flat or drifting. Volatility is minimal. Narratives are stale. Optimism feels misplaced.

This is when Bitcoin quietly transfers from:

- leveraged participants
- short-term traders

- emotionally exhausted holders

to:

- long-term holders
- institutions building positions
- entities with patience and balance-sheet capacity

Accumulation rarely feels like opportunity. It feels like boredom with risk attached.

Power is moving, but price gives no applause.

Phase Two: Compression—When Pressure Builds Invisibly

Compression follows accumulation but often goes unrecognized.

Price remains constrained, yet beneath the surface:

- supply tightens
- liquidity thins
- available sellers are exhausted

At the same time:

- macro pressure builds
- narratives conflict
- volatility compresses

Observers begin to ask:

"Why isn't price reacting to all of this?"

The answer is simple:

Pressure is building, not releasing.

Compression is uncomfortable because nothing appears to happen—until it does.

Phase Three: Ignition—When the Match Appears

Ignition is not caused by a single event.
It is enabled by prior conditions.

A catalyst—rate cuts, liquidity shifts, institutional flows, or policy clarity—acts as a match only because firewood is already stacked.

Price breaks upward decisively.
Volatility returns.
Narratives flip from skeptical to explanatory.

Ignition feels sudden to those focused on price—
and overdue to those who were.

Phase Four: Expansion—When Everyone Understands Bitcoin

Expansion is the most visible phase.

Price accelerates.
Media attention intensifies.
Participation broadens.
Certainty increases.

Fundamentals are rediscovered.
Projections become linear.
Risk is reframed as inevitability.

Power transfers again—from early accumulators to late participants. Expansion is convincing. It is also temporary.

Phase Five: Correction—When Reality Reasserts Itself

Correction is not failure. It is function.

Corrections reset leverage, expose weak structures, and redistribute power.

- Price declines.
- Narratives fracture.
- Confidence evaporates.

Who sells matters far more than how far price falls. Correction completes the cycle and seeds the next accumulation phase.

Why Power Moves in Cycles

This cycle is a framework for understanding how power moves when scarcity, time, and human behavior collide.

Once you see it, you stop asking why price behaves strangely—and start asking who is being forced to act.

Over time, these behaviors begin to form patterns—shaped by incentives, time horizons, and human behavior.
They tend to repeat long before they are widely recognized.

Before examining how pressure eventually converts into movement, it is necessary to understand how to interpret moments when the market appears undecided—when nothing has resolved, but something has clearly changed.

Not every drawdown is a verdict.
Not every pause is a reversal.
Not every stress event represents failure.

Some moments require interpretation before explanation.

Those moments are transitions.

Chapter 5—Transitions, Not Verdicts

Drafted: December 2025

"In the middle of difficulty lies opportunity."
— Albert Einstein

Markets are loudest when clarity is lowest.

Prices move. Narratives multiply. Confidence fractures.
Observers rush to declare meaning—often prematurely.

Not every drawdown is a failure.
Not every pause is a reversal.
Not every stress event delivers a verdict.

Some moments are transitions.

The difference between transition and verdict shapes how stress
is perceived.

Stress Is Information, Not Judgment

Stress reveals how a system behaves under load—where
pressure accumulates, where it dissipates, and where it cannot
pass through.

In traditional markets, stress often forces resolution. Assets are
sold. Leverage unwinds. Weak participants exit. The system
resets.

Bitcoin has begun to behave differently.

Stress no longer guarantees release.

A Common Misread

When markets move sharply, observers instinctively ask:

What broke?

That question assumes something must have failed.

Often, nothing broke.

What changed was pressure.

Macro tightening, liquidity withdrawal, or risk repricing does not invalidate a structure. It tests it. If selling emerges easily, the structure was fragile. If supply remains locked, the structure held.

The market's behavior—not the headline—provides the answer.

Rejection vs. Reset

A rejection is structural.

It occurs when price moves into an area where supply responds decisively. Sellers emerge. Ownership changes hands. Conviction transfers.

A reset is behavioral.

It occurs when pressure exhausts leveraged participants without redistributing underlying supply. Volatility resolves, but ownership remains largely unchanged.

Bitcoin has begun to experience resets more frequently than rejections.

Exhaustion is not the same as failure.

Why Volatility Persists Without Resolution

In systems with constrained supply, volatility can persist without producing outcomes observers expect.

Price may move sharply without triggering selling. Drawdowns may occur without redistribution. Recoveries may happen without renewed enthusiasm.

This conflicts with expectations formed in legacy market behavior.

The absence of resolution can signal constraint rather than weakness.

Wicks, Pauses, and Silence

Sharp intraday moves—both up and down—are often interpreted as decisive signals.

They rarely are.

Wicks represent attempts by price to locate supply or demand. When those attempts fail, price retreats—not because the thesis broke, but because it remains unresolved.

Pauses serve a similar function. They are moments where pressure accumulates without release.

Silence is not absence.
It is compression.

Why This Matters Before Liquidity

Before discussing liquidity and credit, it helps to clarify one assumption: markets don't always resolve tension through selling.

They do not.

Some systems absorb tension until resolution becomes unavoidable—and discontinuous.

This does not make it predictable.
It makes it interpretable.

Behavior During Transition

During transitional periods, markets tend to exhibit the following behaviors:

- Focus on ownership, not price
- Observe supply response, not volatility
- Distinguish stress absorption from distribution
- Resist narrative urgency

CME Gaps: A Transitional Artifact, Not a Verdict

When Bitcoin futures markets pause for weekends, price may move elsewhere. The difference between the last futures close and the next open is called a CME gap. These gaps sometimes close, sometimes don't—they reflect the seam between continuous and scheduled markets, not directional forecasts.

Where Interpretation Ends and Constraint Begins

Transitions describe moments of uncertainty. They don't determine outcomes.

But interpretation has limits.

When pressure persists, ambiguity does not resolve through narratives, sentiment, or belief. It resolves through constraint. At that point, the question is no longer how to read the market, *but* what the market is able to do.

The next chapter shifts the lens outward.

Not to explain Bitcoin through macro conditions—but to show how macro pressure interacts with a market whose supply no longer responds as expected. Liquidity, rates, inflation, and policy do not *cause* what follows. They apply force to a system already constrained.

When interpretation gives way to constraint, outcomes are no longer ambiguous.

Macro does not create scarcity.
It reveals what scarcity does when pressure arrives.

Chapter 6—Macro Is Pressure, Not Cause

Drafted: December 2025

"Stress does not create character.
It reveals it."
— John Wooden

Macroeconomic conditions are often treated as explanations.
They function more like stress tests.

Interest rates, liquidity levels, currency movements, inflation,
policy decisions, and banking mechanics do not create Bitcoin
cycles. They apply pressure to structures that already exist.

What breaks—or what suddenly accelerates—was already weak
or already prepared long before that pressure appeared.

Macro does not determine outcomes.
It reveals them.

Why Macro Gets Too Much Credit

When markets move sharply, explanations arrive immediately.

A central bank decision.
A CPI report.
An election result.
A move in the dollar.

Headlines assemble these into a story that feels causal—clean,
legible, and reassuring. They suggest that markets respond
predictably to discrete events, and that watching the right
variable at the right moment is enough.

Markets rarely move that way.

Large moves occur when conditions quietly mature and pressure finally finds a release point. Macro events are often the moment a move becomes visible. They are rarely the reason it was possible.

Pressure vs. Structure

Think of macro pressure like weight being added to a bridge.

If the bridge is sound, it holds.
If it is strained, cracks appear.

The weight did not create the weakness.
It exposed it.

Bitcoin behaves the same way.

When supply is constrained and ownership is strong, pressure is absorbed. When ownership is fragile, pressure creates fractures. Macro pressure does not decide which outcome occurs.
Structure does.

The Yield Curve: A Signal, Not a Switch

The yield curve compares short-term and long-term interest rates. It reflects how much the government must pay to borrow for a few months versus many years.

In normal conditions, long-term borrowing pays more than short-term borrowing. Lending for longer periods carries more uncertainty, so investors demand higher compensation. Credit flows, refinancing remains available, and the system operates without visible strain.

An inverted yield curve appears when short-term rates rise above long-term rates. That inversion signals discomfort about the near future. Investors favor flexibility and safety over long commitments. Credit becomes harder to roll. Liquidity slows.

This does not break the system immediately.
It restricts it.

The yield curve is not an on/off switch. Inversion does not end cycles, and re-steepening does not ignite them. An inverted curve acts as a headwind. A steepening curve removes that headwind—but does not supply fuel.

Pressure may ease. Movement still depends on structure.

Liquidity: The Macro Variable That Matters Most

Among all macro variables, liquidity shapes outcomes most directly.

Liquidity refers to how easily money can move—how readily capital can be deployed, borrowed, or repositioned without friction.

Liquidity determines:

- how freely capital flows
- how quickly risk is repriced
- how long leverage can persist

Bitcoin responds asymmetrically to liquidity.

When liquidity loosens, upside tends to accelerate.
When liquidity tightens, weaker holders are tested first.

Liquidity alone does not cause repricing.
It converts existing constraints into motion.

Without constrained supply, liquidity mostly creates noise.
With constrained supply, liquidity creates velocity.

Where Liquidity Actually Comes From

Liquidity is not sentiment. It is mechanical.

It originates on central-bank balance sheets.

When central banks buy assets, lend to banks, or open funding facilities, reserves are injected into the system. When those programs are reduced or reversed, liquidity is withdrawn.

Interest rates influence behavior at the margins.
Balance sheets determine whether capital is abundant or scarce in the first place.

Liquidity rarely arrives with a single announcement. It moves quietly—through banks, funding markets, and institutions—long before it becomes obvious to the public.

Why Liquidity Is Global

Central banks are national institutions, but liquidity does not stay local.

Capital moves freely across borders. When money becomes easier to access in one major system, it flows outward. When it tightens, pressure builds globally.

The U.S. dollar plays a central role because so much global trade, debt, and finance is denominated in dollars. Dollar liquidity affects financial conditions almost everywhere at once.

Other major central banks—the European Central Bank, the Bank of Japan, and the People's Bank of China—operate within the same interconnected system. Their actions may push or pull in different directions, but the result is a single global liquidity environment.

This is why Bitcoin responds to global conditions rather than what is happening in any one country.

Liquidity Moves Before You Hear About It

Liquidity moves before it becomes obvious.

By the time easing is widely discussed, prices have often already moved. Bitcoin is especially sensitive to this process because it trades globally, continuously, and without intermediaries.

Liquidity does not announce itself.
It reveals itself through behavior.

Liquidity Doesn't Switch On. It Loosens.

Liquidity is often described as a switch—on or off. That framing misses the most important part of the cycle.

Liquidity does not arrive all at once. It loosens gradually as pressure recedes and circulation resumes. Markets do not move directly from restrictive to expansive. They pass through a narrow transition zone that is quiet, easily overlooked, and decisive.

At one end of the spectrum, conditions are restrictive. Cash is scarce. Pullbacks extend. Volatility persists because liquidity cannot absorb stress.

At the other end, conditions are loose. Prices rise easily. Volatility collapses. Bad news stops working.

Between those states is a middle ground—where conditions are no longer tightening but not yet expansive. Markets function. Stress is contained. Capital remains cautious.

This is where cycles turn.

The critical shift is not from restrictive to euphoric. It is from constrained to permissive—the point where markets begin to move before policy changes are announced, before headlines catch up, and before consensus feels comfortable.

This transition does not require dramatic intervention.
It requires circulation.

When cash accumulates at the central bank—through bond issuance, taxation, or similar mechanisms—liquidity tightens because that money is inert. It does not circulate or express itself through risk.

Liquidity begins to loosen when that cash moves back into the system through spending, transfers, payments, or interest flows.

No new money needs to be created.
Conditions simply stop getting tighter and begin getting easier.

When that threshold is crossed, behavior changes before narratives do. Pullbacks attract buyers. Volatility falls even as prices rise. Negative headlines lose their ability to push markets lower.

This is not euphoria.
It is early expansion.

Why Bitcoin Reacts So Sharply

Most assets absorb liquidity slowly. Earnings, dividends, and cash flows act as shock absorbers.

Bitcoin does not have those.

It has:

- a fixed supply
- a relatively small amount actually available for sale
- no issuer
- no yield holding price in place

When liquidity expands into a market where supply is already tight, price does not drift higher.
It jumps.

Liquidity does not create Bitcoin's value.
It determines when that value appears in price.

Liquidity supplies the energy.
Supply constraint turns it into velocity.

When liquidity meets scarce supply, the effect compounds. Rising price changes behavior. Long-term holders become less willing to sell. New participants arrive. Sellable supply shrinks further.

By the time liquidity is obvious, the supply response is already working against late entrants.

Macro as Pressure, Liquidity as Access

Macro becomes decisive only when conditions are already set.

Rate cuts do not cause repricing on their own. They matter only when supply is constrained, sellers are largely exhausted, and liquidity is positioned to move.

In those conditions, macro supplies the permission structure.
Liquidity supplies the energy.

That is why similar macro events produce wildly different outcomes across cycles.

The data did not change.
The structure did.

Why This Matters Now

Macro discussion intensifies when outcomes are unclear.

That is not coincidence.
It is compression.

When supply is tight and pressure is building, people search for explanations. Macro fills the narrative gap.

What matters is not predicting macro events.
It is understanding what breaks—or accelerates—when pressure finally finds release.

The next chapter examines what happens when liquidity continues to circulate through a system that no longer releases sellable supply—and why, under those conditions, adjustment cannot remain gradual.

Chapter 7—Liquidity Without Exit

Drafted: December 2025

"The problem is not that liquidity disappears. It's that it appears where there is no escape."
— Author Unknown

The Old Assumption

For years, financial markets followed a familiar rhythm. When liquidity increased, asset prices generally rose. When it tightened, prices tended to fall. And when things went wrong, holders could usually sell and move on.

That pattern has quietly faded.

Not because markets changed overnight, but because one asset changed how liquidity interacts with the system.

Bitcoin converts capital into long-duration holding by making supply less likely to return once acquired.

Liquidity Is No Longer Mobile

In conventional finance, liquidity behaved like water. Capital flowed from cash to bonds, from bonds to stocks, from stocks to real estate, and back again as conditions shifted.

Nearly everything was tradable. Markets usually had depth. Assets almost always found a buyer in time.

Bitcoin breaks that cycle.

Not because Bitcoin is hard to buy—the market remains liquid on entry—but because supply increasingly does not return once acquired.

Coins are moved into long-term storage, professional custody, treasury reserves, or collateral arrangements. There is little need to sell, reinvest elsewhere, or rebalance constantly. Those coins largely stop participating in day-to-day trading.

Liquidity enters Bitcoin with ease.
Sellable supply rarely flows back out.

The Absorption Mechanism

This absorption occurs through several overlapping channels. Long-term individual holders remove coins from exchanges. Corporations building Bitcoin into their balance sheets do the same. ETFs place coins into regulated custody structures designed for duration. Borrowers increasingly pledge Bitcoin as collateral rather than selling it.

Each channel reduces tradable supply without immediately creating new sellers.

This does not mean supply is permanently removed. Under stress—credit contraction, regulatory pressure, or liquidity crisis—coins can and will return to market.

But absent forced conditions, structurally held Bitcoin tends to remain dormant for extended periods.

Most models assume rising prices will eventually draw supply back into the market. In Bitcoin, that response appears to weaken as collateralization and institutional duration increase. Capital arrives, demand builds, yet large-scale sellable supply has re-emerged less reliably in recent cycles.

If that behavior reverses at scale, the compression thesis fails visibly.

Why Credit Changes Everything

A significant shift in this cycle is the rise of Bitcoin-backed credit.

Historically, rising prices encouraged selling—to cover taxes, fund expenses, rebalance portfolios, or lock in gains near perceived peaks. Selling was the mechanism that returned supply to the market.

Bitcoin-backed credit interrupts that pattern.

Holders can now access liquidity without selling their Bitcoin. They avoid selling into rallies, avoid liquidating to fund daily needs, and avoid exiting simply because prices feel "high." Loans can be rolled forward or refinanced instead.

This changes Bitcoin's role. Volatility can be collateralized. Appreciation becomes usable without disposal.

Credit is not liquidity itself—it is how liquidity is accessed.

The New Instruments Reducing Sellable Bitcoin

Bitcoin doesn't need to be locked up to become unavailable. It only needs owners who no longer need to sell.

That shift is already underway, driven by a growing set of financial instruments designed to raise liquidity without liquidating Bitcoin. These tools don't change Bitcoin's total supply. They change its behavior.

The common thread is simple: selling is being replaced by financing.

Bitcoin-Anchored Fixed-Income Instruments

A new class of fixed-income-like securities has emerged that allows issuers to raise capital while keeping Bitcoin on their balance sheets.

These instruments—preferred equity, notes, long-duration obligations—allow capital raises while Bitcoin remains on balance sheets. Capital is raised. Obligations are met. Bitcoin remains untouched.

From a market perspective, that Bitcoin still exists—but it no longer functions as tradable inventory.

Collateralized Refinancing

Bitcoin is increasingly used as collateral for refinancing rather than sold.

In this model, Bitcoin is pledged to raise liquidity, loans are rolled or extended, and obligations are managed without liquidation. This is how mature assets behave in established financial systems. Real estate is refinanced far more often than it is sold.

Once Bitcoin enters this role, it becomes economically inactive from a selling standpoint. It's visible, but unavailable.

Credit Substitutes for Selling — Under Conditions

Credit does not eliminate selling.
It substitutes for selling under specific structural conditions.

Bitcoin-backed financing only displaces supply if:

- Loan-to-value ratios remain conservative (often 30–35% in durable credit systems)

- Lenders maintain confidence in Bitcoin as high-quality collateral
- Volatility remains within acceptable margin thresholds

If those conditions deteriorate, liquidation can re-enter the system. In that case, selling resumes its historical role in restoring market balance.

Balance-Sheet Reserve Structures

As Bitcoin moves onto long-term balance sheets, new securities form around it. These instruments are not designed to trade Bitcoin. They are designed to preserve it while allowing liquidity to exist elsewhere in the structure.

At this stage, selling becomes less necessary. Financing replaces liquidation. Duration replaces turnover.

What This Changes

None of these instruments lock Bitcoin on-chain or remove it from custody. They simply remove it from the decision to sell.

That distinction matters.

Markets don't price total supply. They price available supply. As Bitcoin shifts from something that must be sold to something that can be financed against, sellable supply shrinks quietly, well before price moves make it obvious.

This is how supply tightens without drama—and why, over time, selling stops making sense.

Stablecoins: Liquidity in Waiting

Another structural shift complicates traditional liquidity models: the rise of stablecoins.

Stablecoins function as digital dollar equivalents held within the crypto ecosystem. They do not represent new Bitcoin demand by themselves. They represent liquidity positioned for deployment.

In prior cycles, capital often had to move from traditional banking rails into exchanges before it could purchase Bitcoin. Today, large pools of dollar-denominated liquidity already reside on-chain, inside exchanges, custody platforms, and decentralized finance systems.

This changes timing.

Stablecoin balances can expand significantly without immediately affecting Bitcoin's price. They accumulate quietly, waiting for opportunity, volatility, or narrative alignment. When deployed, they do not need to clear traditional banking friction. They convert into Bitcoin instantly.

Stablecoins do not reduce sellable supply. They amplify demand velocity.

This distinction matters.

If Bitcoin supply is increasingly held in long-duration structures, while dollar liquidity accumulates in stablecoin form, liquidity expansion does not simply raise prices gradually. It can accelerate repricing when dormant capital moves against constrained supply.

Stablecoins are not Bitcoin liquidity.

They are liquidity positioned against Bitcoin.

And when liquidity meets shrinking available supply, price does not adjust smoothly. It compresses, then moves.

The Exit Door Is Narrowing

Traditional markets rely on the expectation that higher prices will attract sellers.

Bitcoin steadily undermines that expectation.

Over time, holding periods lengthen, willing sellers diminish, and circulating supply shrinks. New buyers compete for a smaller tradable float, much of which is held by committed owners or locked inside institutional custody and credit structures.

Liquidity can still move price upward.
It can no longer reliably draw supply back into the market.

This is not a dramatic short squeeze with a single breaking point. It is quieter and more durable: structural illiquidity building over time.

Divergence and the Decision Not to Sell

By the time divergence becomes visible, behavior has already changed.

People don't stop selling because they expect prices to rise. They stop selling because selling no longer solves the problem they're trying to escape.

In a diverging system, effort, wages, and productivity lose their ability to reliably preserve value across time. Progress continues, but it no longer reconciles with lived experience. The result is not panic—it is caution.

The central question shifts quietly:
Not "How do I optimize returns?"
But "What can I hold that won't force me backward?"

That shift is decisive.

When capital begins prioritizing certainty over yield, time horizons extend. Assets that depend on flexibility, policy intervention, or expanding supply feel less reliable. Assets governed by fixed rules and indifferent to economic narratives feel more stable—even when their prices fluctuate.

This is why divergence tightens supply before it increases demand.

Selling becomes harder to justify. Volatility becomes tolerable. Ownership becomes defensive rather than speculative.

What looks like patience often reflects underlying pressure.

As more holders reach the same conclusion independently, available supply recedes without coordination or announcement. Nothing dramatic needs to happen. The market simply becomes thinner.

When liquidity eventually arrives—whether through stimulus, allocation shifts, or narrative alignment—it encounters a market that is already thinner. Moves become faster not because enthusiasm suddenly appears, but because resistance quietly disappeared earlier.

This is why divergence matters structurally. It does not ignite movement. It prepares conditions that alter how repricing occurs once pressure converts into movement.

Why This Isn't a Bubble

Classic bubbles rely on easy entry and the expectation of easy exit.

Bitcoin still offers relatively easy entry. Easy exit, however, is steadily disappearing.

That asymmetry changes everything.

Panic selling, cascading exits, and forced liquidation—the hallmarks of bubbles—lose their power when large holders no longer need or want to sell. Older cycle frameworks struggle precisely because they depend on selling pressure that no longer appears at scale.

401(k)s: When Allocation Becomes Automatic

Most capital does not move because of conviction.
It moves because of defaults.

Retirement systems are built on inertia. Contributions occur through payroll deduction. Allocations are set automatically. Rebalancing happens without active decision-making. Participants rarely select individual assets. They accept the structure provided.

This matters because it changes how demand enters the market.

When Bitcoin becomes available inside retirement plans— whether directly, through exchange-traded products, or as part of diversified allocation models—capital does not arrive because investors "decide" to buy Bitcoin. It arrives because the system allocates exposure by default.

This is a structural shift.

A worker does not wake up and time an entry. Bitcoin is allocated quietly, repeatedly, and over long time horizons.

These flows are fundamentally different from speculative demand. They are not sensitive to short-term price movements. They do not respond emotionally to volatility. They arrive steadily, independent of narrative or sentiment.

Within retirement systems, Bitcoin functions as reserve exposure beneath the portfolio, similar to how inflation hedges, duration offsets, or strategic diversifiers are treated today.

Once embedded in retirement infrastructure, selling becomes less common—not because selling is prohibited, but because it becomes unnecessary. Exposure accumulates passively. Time replaces timing.

As allocation becomes automatic, one assumption quietly breaks: that rising prices must eventually force selling.

In systems governed by defaults rather than discretion, accumulation persists even when price fluctuates. Over time, this changes the character of the market itself.

The Market Hasn't Priced This In

Most valuation models still assume routine profit-taking, portfolio rebalancing, clean cycle tops, and eventual mean reversion. All those assumptions depend on supply returning to the market as prices rise.

Bitcoin is steadily removing that supply.

The process is gradual, not sudden. But each cycle begins with less freely available Bitcoin than the one before it.

When liquidity expands again—and it will—it will encounter a market with a smaller tradable supply, stronger holders, widespread institutional custody, and borrowers with little incentive to sell.

The result will not resemble a classic speculative blow-off top. It will resemble a repricing.

Not because demand suddenly explodes, but because exit liquidity no longer exists at meaningful scale.

Understanding the "Liquidity Sink"
(Beginner Note)

In simple terms, liquidity refers to how easily money and credit can move through the financial system.

A sink absorbs what flows into it without letting much flow back out.

Bitcoin increasingly behaves this way.

Liquidity flows in through individual purchases, institutional allocations, ETFs, corporate treasuries, and lending platforms. But once Bitcoin enters long-term ownership—cold storage, balance sheets, custody, or collateral—it rarely returns to active circulation.

Traditional assets recycle supply when prices rise. Bitcoin increasingly does not. The tradable float keeps shrinking relative to potential demand.

That one-way absorption is what makes Bitcoin a liquidity sink—and why expansions in liquidity now behave very differently than older models expect.

This Is the Trap

The financial system must inject liquidity to function.

• It can direct liquidity into Bitcoin.
• It cannot easily retrieve Bitcoin.
• It cannot force widespread selling.
• And it cannot reprice gradually.

When that structural reality becomes visible, price discovery accelerates—not from speculation or excitement, but from necessity.

Chapter 7 Summary

Bitcoin is no longer simply another asset competing within markets.
It has become a liquidity sink.

Capital can enter.
Sellable supply does not freely return.

That shift quietly reshapes everything that follows.

When exit liquidity disappears, markets do not simply become illiquid. They become unstable in a different way. Prices can still move—but they move under constraint. They do not adjust smoothly. They reprice.

What follows is not a familiar cycle of excess and correction, but a period where pressure builds quietly, with no obvious release valve—until it finally expresses itself.

Ignition follows.

Not because of sentiment, narratives, or timing models—but because pressure eventually exhausts every alternative.

Chapter 8—Ignition

Drafted: December 2025

"The most dangerous moment is when pressure finally looks like motion."
— Author Unknown

For long stretches, nothing appears to happen.

Structural pressure builds quietly. Liquidity accumulates. Sellable supply tightens and ownership hardens. The structure becomes increasingly rigid, while price remains deceptively calm. To observers, the market looks dormant. To skeptics, it looks exhausted. To those waiting for a familiar cycle, it looks late.

Then something changes—not in sentiment, but in constraint.

Not because a story emerges. Not because a prediction comes true. But because the system reaches a point where pressure can no longer be absorbed invisibly.

That moment is ignition.

Ignition is not a narrative event. It is not an announcement. It is not a policy decision or a headline. It is the point at which a structurally constrained market is forced to express itself through price.

And when it happens, it feels sudden.

When Sellers Disappear

In traditional markets, rising prices eventually bring sellers back. Profit-taking increases. Supply returns. The move slows. That release valve is assumed to exist.

In Bitcoin, that assumption increasingly fails.

By the time ignition occurs, most weak holders have already exited. Coins are held by long-duration owners, institutional custody structures, balance sheets, and collateral arrangements. Selling is no longer the default response to rising prices. Often, it is not necessary at all.

So when new demand arrives, it does not meet a wall of supply. It meets silence.

That is ignition.

Price does not rise because enthusiasm explodes. It rises because the market discovers that there is far less available Bitcoin than expected. Bids stack. Offers thin. Small moves begin to travel farther than models predict.

What looks like momentum is often just absence.

Why Ignition Feels Violent

Ignition rarely unfolds smoothly.

After extended compression, even modest liquidity can produce outsized movement. Gaps appear where continuous trading once existed. Resistance levels that seemed meaningful are crossed with little friction. Price moves not in steps, but in jolts.

This is why ignition is often described as parabolic in hindsight, even when it didn't feel euphoric in real time. The market is not accelerating because participants are irrational. It is accelerating because structure has removed the brakes.

Importantly, ignition does not require universal agreement. It often begins while doubt remains widespread. Many participants hesitate, waiting for pullbacks that never arrive. Others attempt to fade the move, expecting a familiar reversal.

Those expectations are rooted in older market behavior.

Ignition breaks them.

Liquidity Meets Constraint

This is the moment when liquidity meets a market that no longer offers exit at scale. At ignition, the full weight of constrained supply is finally revealed.

Capital that had been waiting on the sidelines re-enters. New buyers arrive, not because of belief, but because price is already moving. Institutions that require confirmation see enough evidence to act. Systems that rebalance mechanically begin to allocate.

None of this is dramatic in isolation.

Together, it overwhelms a market with no easy exits.

Liquidity does not flood in all at once. But each incremental inflow has a larger effect than the last, because it is competing for a shrinking pool of sellable supply. The result is reflexive: price movement attracts attention, attention attracts capital, and capital encounters constraint.

Ignition is not the cause of the loop—it is the moment it becomes visible.

Why This Isn't the Top

Ignition is often mistaken for the end.

Sharp moves trigger memories of past peaks. Commentators warn of excess. Comparisons are made to bubbles and blow-offs. Calls for caution multiply.

But ignition is not excess. It is exposure.

It reveals how little supply is actually available. It exposes how outdated many assumptions have become. And it highlights the difference between a market driven by speculation and one driven by structural imbalance.

True excess requires widespread leverage, eager sellers, and easy exits. Ignition has none of those.

Once ignition occurs, the market cannot return to its prior state.

Price has moved far enough to change perception. Ownership has become more visible. Participation broadens. New frameworks are applied. Institutions and regulators take notice. Narratives shift from "if" to "how."

What follows is not a return to normal volatility, but a new phase where Bitcoin is treated differently—by markets, by capital, and by the system itself. Ignition does not resolve pressure. It transfers it into the open.

Chapter 9 explores what happens once that pressure is no longer hidden—how expansion unfolds, why repricing replaces cycling, and why the old four-year framework begins to fail

under the weight of a market that no longer offers an exit on
demand.

Chapter 9—Expansion

Drafted: December 2025

"What changes markets is not belief. It is participation."
— Author Unknown

Ignition makes price visible.
Expansion makes it unavoidable.

Once Bitcoin moves far enough without retracing, the character of the market changes. Attention broadens. Participation widens. Frameworks that once dismissed Bitcoin are forced to engage with it—not as a curiosity, but as a factor that must be accounted for.

Expansion is not the fastest part of the move.
It is the widest.

From Signal to Participation

In the early stages after ignition, price movement alone is the message. Expansion begins when that signal spreads beyond early observers.

Participants who require confirmation start to act—not because they believe, but because the cost of ignoring Bitcoin has risen. Models are updated. Mandates are revisited. Exposure that was once optional becomes defensible.

This is how expansion works.
Not through persuasion, but through permission.

As participation broadens, volume increases, volatility becomes two-sided, and pullbacks begin to appear. These are not signs of weakness. They are signs that the market is deepening.

Bitcoin is no longer trading in isolation.
It is being incorporated.

A Different Kind of Volatility

During expansion, volatility changes character.

Moves are still sharp, but they are no longer driven solely by the absence of sellers. They are driven by disagreement—between those entering late, those holding long, and those attempting to impose older frameworks onto a market that no longer behaves the same way.

Corrections occur. Narratives fluctuate. Confidence is tested.

But something important does not happen.
Supply does not meaningfully return.

Holders who endured ignition have little incentive to sell. Institutions entering through custody, funds, or balance sheets are not trading tactically. Borrowers using Bitcoin as collateral are not exiting.

Each pullback is met not with liquidation, but with absorption.

Expansion is noisy.
It is not fragile.

The Clearance Price

At some point during expansion, price reaches a level that draws out illiquid supply—Bitcoin held by long-duration owners who were never part of the active market.

Liquid supply trades constantly. Illiquid supply appears only when price overcomes time horizon, conviction, and alternative options such as collateralization.

The clearance price is not a target.
It is not predictable in advance.
It does not arrive with an announcement.

It is simply the price at which hardened holders—those with long time horizons and strong conviction—become willing to part with meaningful amounts of Bitcoin.

Until that level is reached, price can rise with relatively little resistance. Once it is reached, selling increases, volatility intensifies, and market behavior changes.

Clearance pricing does not make liquidity return. It forces a small number of long-term holders to sell when they otherwise would not.

Models underestimate this process because they assume supply responds mechanically to price. In Bitcoin, supply responds psychologically—and often only after years of reinforcement.

The clearance price does not mark the end of expansion.
It marks the first real test of it.

Recognition Follows Price

One of the defining features of expansion is recognition.

Media coverage shifts tone. Language changes. Bitcoin is no longer discussed as a speculative fringe, but as a market factor.

This recognition is not celebratory.
It is procedural.

As participation grows, the system begins formalizing what it can no longer ignore.

This is where law enters—not as a catalyst, but as a response.

When the Law Shows Up

Large changes in finance rarely start with laws. They begin when behavior changes first.

By the time lawmakers act, markets have already moved. Capital has repositioned. Infrastructure has formed.

As digital custody, credit, and settlement expand, regulators are forced to clarify rules that were once theoretical. Questions of custody, reserves, balance-sheet treatment, and responsibility must be answered because institutions cannot operate at scale without clarity.

This process does not tame Bitcoin.
It reveals its role.

As upper layers of the financial system become more regulated and policy-driven, the value of a neutral, non-discretionary asset beneath them becomes clearer.

Bitcoin is not pulled into the system as a payment tool.
It is positioned beneath it as a reserve and collateral layer.

The law does not legitimize Bitcoin.
It adapts around it.

Expansion Feels Unstable

Expansion is often uncomfortable.

Participation widens faster than understanding. Narratives multiply. Confidence swings. Volatility increases even as conviction strengthens. Observers struggle to reconcile old models with new behavior.

This tension leads many to assume the system is fragile.
It is not.

What feels like instability is structural adjustment. The market is discovering where supply actually lies, how much demand exists, and which assumptions no longer apply.

Expansion is the phase where older cycle logic begins to break down—not in theory, but in practice.

The Cycle Under Pressure

The traditional four-year cycle assumes predictable supply response, routine profit-taking, clear tops and bottoms, and clean resets.

Expansion undermines those assumptions.

As supply hardens, exit liquidity diminishes, and participation extends into institutions, the cycle loses symmetry. Moves stretch. Corrections compress. Timing becomes less obvious.

This does not eliminate volatility.
It changes its purpose.

When markets no longer clear through routine profit-taking, cycles lose their organizing role. Volatility no longer signals repetition—it signals constraint.

What follows is not the end of cycles as movement, but the end of cycles as a reliable framework.

Chapter 10 examines why the familiar cycle model fails under these conditions—and what replaces it when scarcity, credit, and institutional behavior reshape market logic.

Chapter 10—Beyond the Four-Year Cycle

Drafted: December 2025

"There is no more crypto winter."
— Michael Saylor

Why the Four-Year Cycle Once Made Sense

For most of Bitcoin's history, the four-year cycle was a useful framework for understanding market behavior.

A halving reduced new supply. Scarcity became visible. Price rose. Early holders sold into strength. Excess leverage accumulated. Eventually, capitulation reset the market.

Coins were redistributed from early adopters to new entrants, and from weaker hands to stronger ones. Each cycle ended with reduced conviction, high volatility, and a circulating supply that remained broadly tradeable.

The model worked because selling was necessary.

What Bitcoin Halvings Were Designed to Do

Bitcoin issues new coins as a reward to miners for securing the network. Roughly every four years, that reward is cut in half. This event is called a halving.

The intention was deliberate: Bitcoin's supply would slow down in predictable steps rather than all at once.

In Bitcoin's early years, halvings had powerful effects. Each one sharply reduced the flow of new coins entering the market while demand continued to grow. With fewer new coins available, prices tended to rise.

This produced a familiar progression:

- A halving reduced new supply
- Scarcity became noticeable
- Price increased
- Early holders sold into strength
- Excess leverage formed
- A sharp correction followed

The market reset, and the cycle began again.

This worked because new supply still mattered, and because selling was the only way holders could access liquidity. Halvings acted as clear starting points for each new phase. That mechanism shaped Bitcoin's early history and trained participants to expect cycles.

What changed is not the halving itself.
What changed is everything around it.

What the Cycle Required

The four-year framework depended on three conditions:

- Sellers had to emerge at higher prices
- Profit-taking had to redistribute supply
- Capitulation had to reset conviction

Without these elements, the cycle loses its symmetry and becomes something else.

Bitcoin is no longer reliably meeting all three conditions at scale.

Cycle Erosion Is Conditional

The erosion of the four-year cycle is not guaranteed.

It depends on whether structural holders continue to dominate reflexive sellers.

If long-term holder supply contracts during future halvings instead of expanding, the reset mechanism weakens.

If forced liquidation reappears at scale—through leverage expansion, credit fragility, or macro stress—the cycle can reassert.

The halving has not disappeared.
What changes is the environment in which it operates.

In a prolonged credit contraction, even structurally held Bitcoin can be mobilized. In that Market State, credit tightens, haircuts widen, and forced selling can re-enter.

Why Selling No Longer Occurs at Scale

As shown in earlier chapters, holders increasingly understand that selling Bitcoin is a one-way decision.

Once Bitcoin became collateralizable, institutionally custodied, and usable as balance-sheet capital, selling stopped being required to access liquidity.

Credit/hoarding circularity

This is the same core critique as Claude.

You already improved this with the conditional LTV framing—but we can add one more sentence to fully close the loop:

Add one "independent bootstrapping" line:

- ETF/treasury programs
- ongoing on-chain adoption/custody infrastructure

- balance-sheet accounting treatment
- persistent demand flows not dependent on price reflexivity

Example line:

Credit substitution is reinforced not only by conviction, but by institutional structures that continue operating through volatility—custody rails, treasury policies, and long-duration mandates.

That breaks the "conviction is the only support" loop.

That shift quietly undermines the old cycle model.

Permanent Hoarders Break the Rhythm

Permanent hoarders treat Bitcoin as non-saleable reserve collateral rather than an asset to rotate out of portfolios.

The four-year cycle assumed that rising prices would eventually force selling. Permanent hoarders weaken that assumption.

They do not sell because they do not need to. They can borrow without forfeiting ownership, and they understand that re-entry risk is asymmetric—what they sell may not be recoverable at scale.

This removes the mechanism that once produced blow-off tops, violent retracements, and long winters.

Cycles require exhaustion.
Permanent hoarders do not exhaust.

Why Halvings May Matter Less as Collateralization Grows

Halvings still matter, but no longer as resets.

Originally, halvings reduced new supply, accelerated scarcity, and triggered speculative cycles. Today, halvings occur inside a market where circulating supply is already constrained, selling pressure is structurally reduced, and demand is increasingly institutional and persistent.

Halvings no longer start cycles.
They intensify imbalance.

Why "Winter" Required Capitulation

A winter was never simply a period of low prices. It required forced selling—over-leverage, margin calls, insolvency, and psychological surrender.

Bitcoin's ownership base has changed.

Today's holders generally carry little or no leverage, use Bitcoin as collateral rather than margin, and are under no obligation to sell.

Without forced liquidation at scale, "winter" becomes less about capitulation and more about consolidation.

This May Be a Market Phase Change—But It Must Be Earned

Markets treat deviations as temporary. This appears different.

It reflects a structural shift: supply hardening, credit substituting for liquidation, institutional custody extending time horizons, and balance-sheet behavior becoming more common.

The halving still reduces new supply.
What has changed is how little supply returns.

The four-year cycle was a feature of Bitcoin's adolescence.
What follows resembles adulthood.

What Replaces the Four-Year Cycle

Bitcoin does not become stable.
It becomes directional.

Instead of boom, bust, and reset, the pattern shifts toward accumulation, repricing, and consolidation.

Volatility still exists, but it increasingly clusters upward. Corrections still occur, but they do not reliably redistribute supply. Price no longer resets conviction. It reveals scarcity.

Why Many Will Miss This

The four-year cycle is comforting. It offers familiar timing, predictable narratives, and the reassurance that there will always be another entry.

Letting go requires accepting that past maps no longer apply, re-entry may not be available at scale, and waiting can carry its own risk.

This is why many will continue to expect a winter that behaves the way it used to.

What Michael Saylor Meant

When Michael Saylor said there is no more crypto winter, he was not predicting uninterrupted price appreciation.

He was describing a mechanism: the process that once forced Bitcoin to reset through capitulation has been structurally weakened.

Fewer forced sellers.
Less redistribution.
Less reset.

Chapter 10 Summary

The four-year cycle depended on selling.
Selling has increasingly been replaced by hoarding.
Hoarding has been reinforced by credit.
Credit reduces capitulation.

Without capitulation at scale, the traditional cycle loses its function.

Bitcoin's prior rhythm is no longer structurally guaranteed.

Once cycles lose their ability to reset markets, a new question emerges: If Bitcoin no longer resets through selling, where does the next buyer come from?

The answer is not retail.
It is not traders.
Increasingly, it is balance sheets.

Chapter 11 examines how states, institutions, and geopolitical incentives enter a system that no longer releases supply—and why their arrival permanently changes the stakes.

Chapter 11—The Sovereign Layer

Drafted: December 2025

"Nations don't adopt technologies.
They adopt advantages."

— Author Unknown

The sovereign layer is the most speculative component of this framework.

It is not assumed — it is conditional.

If sovereign accumulation fails to materialize or reverses under geopolitical pressure, the structural compression thesis weakens materially.

This chapter outlines possibility — not inevitability.

Treat what follows as a map of incentives—not a forecast that states must accumulate Bitcoin.

Unlike exchange data or custody trends, sovereign behavior is hard to observe in real time and can shift with politics, war, and policy regimes.

This chapter carries the most uncertainty in the book.

Why Sovereigns Arrive Late

Sovereigns are never early.

- They do not speculate.
- They do not evangelize.

- They do not experiment publicly.

They observe.

Nation-states enter only after:

- volatility has meaning
- infrastructure has hardened
- custody has matured
- exit risk has been absorbed by others

Bitcoin now approaches that threshold.

Not because it is fashionable, but because it has become strategically advantageous.

Sovereign Balance-Sheet Implications

Bitcoin does not replace fiat money, Treasury markets, or fiscal discipline.

That's not how this works.

A more realistic way to think about Bitcoin is as a balance-sheet asset, not a currency to be spent.

If a sovereign were to build a meaningful Bitcoin reserve, Bitcoin would not be used to pay national debt.

It would be used the same way durable assets are used everywhere else: as collateral.

The idea is simple:

- Hold a scarce, durable asset
- Borrow conservatively against it
- Avoid selling it

- Refinance over time

Corporations do this with equity.
Individuals do it with real estate.

Bitcoin-backed lending already exists at smaller scale.

Applied carefully, a sovereign Bitcoin reserve could:

- Sit alongside traditional reserves
- Help refinance a portion of debt
- Reduce pressure to monetize at the margins
- Add long-term balance-sheet flexibility

The Sovereign Constraint

Unlike individuals or corporations, sovereigns operate under unique constraints. They must:

- preserve purchasing power
- defend currency credibility
- manage reserves without signaling panic
- move without appearing reactive

This is why sovereign adoption is never loud.

It occurs quietly—through policy language, pilot programs, balance-sheet modeling, and legal groundwork.

By the time it is announced, it has already been decided and acquired.

Why Bitcoin Becomes a Reserve Question

Historically, sovereign reserves relied on:

- gold
- foreign currencies
- treasuries
- strategic commodities

Gold as Historical Precedent — and Structural Limit

Gold has experienced long stagnation phases de++spite scarcity.

Bitcoin differs not because it is scarce — but because it is digitally auditable, instantly transferable, and increasingly integrated into programmable financial infrastructure.

If Bitcoin fails to integrate into credit systems and sovereign accounting frameworks, it risks behaving more like gold's historical stagnation cycles than a structural reserve transition.

Each type of reserve now carries structural limitations:

- gold is immobile
- foreign currencies are politicized
- treasuries are liabilities of other states
- commodities require storage and force

Bitcoin introduces something new: a neutral, bearer, non-sovereign reserve asset that cannot be frozen, diluted, or weaponized.

That combination does not exist elsewhere. .

Bitcoin Is Not Replacing Reserves—It Is Complementing Them

Sovereigns do not need Bitcoin to replace gold or the dollar.

They need it to solve a narrower, more urgent problem:

What reserve asset cannot be controlled by another state?

Bitcoin answers that question cleanly.

At small allocations, it:

- reduces counterparty risk
- adds optionality
- signals technological credibility
- provides asymmetric upside

This is why sovereign adoption begins incrementally.

Why Even Small Sovereign Allocations Matter

Sovereigns do not need large allocations to change the system.

Because Bitcoin's circulating supply is already constrained, even marginal sovereign demand has outsized impact.

A single nation allocating 0.5%, 1%, or less is not making a speculative bet.

It is removing supply permanently.

Sovereigns do not trade reserves.
They accumulate and hold.

This makes them natural permanent hoarders.

The Cost of Inaction

Sovereign states that fail to acquire Bitcoin during its monetization phase are not excluded from the global system.

They are repositioned within it.

Early acting states accumulate quietly, at lower prices, with minimal political cost. Late-acting states face a different reality: thin liquidity, public scrutiny, and acquisition at clearance prices. Once Bitcoin becomes embedded in sovereign balance sheets, there is no wholesale market left to enter discreetly.

The most enduring cost of inaction is not missed upside.

It is permanent asymmetry.

States that hold Bitcoin gain:

- non-politicized collateral
- improved credibility in debt markets
- greater flexibility during currency or liquidity stress

States that do not must rely entirely on fiat credibility and external financing. Over time, this divergence expresses itself quietly through borrowing costs, credit terms, and geopolitical leverage.

Bitcoin does not punish non-adoption.
It simply stops waiting.

Once the window closes, there is no reset, no redistribution, and no second entry cycle. There is only relative positioning—who holds neutral collateral, and who must negotiate without it.

The penalty for delay is not collapse.

It is structural disadvantage.

The First-Mover Advantage Between States

Sovereigns understand something markets often miss:

Reserve assets are positional.

Early accumulation:

- is cheaper
- is less visible
- avoids signaling competition

Late accumulation:

- is expensive
- is public
- forces political justification

This creates a quiet race.

Not to announce adoption—
but to complete it before others do.

Why Sovereigns Deepen Supply Shock

When sovereigns acquire Bitcoin:

- it moves into deep custody
- it exits circulating supply indefinitely
- it becomes politically and strategically untouchable

There is no profit-taking.
There is no cycle trading.
There is no capitulation.

Supply Shock is no longer market driven.

It becomes geopolitical.

The Difference Between Institutional and Sovereign Demand

Institutions allocate for:

- return
- correlation
- portfolio optimization

Sovereigns allocate for:

- power
- resilience
- optionality
- strategic neutrality

This distinction matters.

Institutions may rebalance.
Sovereigns rarely do.

Once Bitcoin enters the sovereign layer,
it becomes structural capital.

Why This Changes Everything

Up to this point, Bitcoin's growth has been absorbed by:

- individuals
- corporations
- funds

Each layer reduced circulating supply.

The sovereign layer does something more consequential:

It removes Bitcoin from history's recycling loop.

Assets that enter sovereign reserves do not come back to market in meaningful size.

They become permanent fixtures of the financial architecture.

Why This Could Become the Most Consequential Layer

There is no higher buyer than a sovereign.

- Retail is optional.
- Institutions are cyclical.
- Funds are tactical.

States are structural.

Once sovereigns begin accumulating Bitcoin:

- supply shock becomes irreversible
- clearance pricing becomes permanent
- the old market framework collapses entirely

At that point, Bitcoin is no longer "emerging."

When Bitcoin enters sovereign balance sheets, the market changes permanently—but not loudly.

There is no announcement that supply has vanished.

No bell signaling a new Market Phase.

No moment where participation suddenly feels closed.

What changes instead is behavior.

- Selling becomes rare.
- Liquidity shifts toward credit.
- Price stops functioning as a clearing mechanism and begins functioning as persuasion.

At that point, the market is no longer discovering Bitcoin.

It is discovering how much conviction it must overcome to acquire it.

Chapter 12 examines that moment—when selling stops being the default response, and price must rise until someone is willing to part with something they believe cannot be replaced.

Chapter 12—When Selling Stops Making Sense

Drafted: December 2025

"When a thing can no longer be replaced,
it is no longer priced—it is rationed."
— Author Unknown

The Moment This Chapter Describes

Most market participants assume selling is always an option.

- They may delay it.
- They may regret it.
- They may mistime it.

But they assume it remains available.

This chapter describes the moment when that assumption breaks—not because rules change, but because reality does.

Selling does not disappear.

It simply stops making sense.

How Markets Normally Clear

In traditional markets, price exists to balance two forces:

Those who want to buy
Those who are willing to sell

When demand rises, price rises—and sellers emerge.
When demand falls, price falls—and buyers appear.

This feedback loop is what allows markets to clear.

Bitcoin is steadily exiting that framework.

Not because demand overwhelms supply in a single moment, but because supply migrates into hands that no longer respond to price.

The Shift From "Asset" to "Property"

An asset is something you plan to exit.

Property is something you plan to hold.

Bitcoin is transitioning from the first category into the second.

This happens when holders internalize a simple realization:

If I sell this, I may never be able to replace it.

- Not at the same price.
- Not in the same quantity.
- Possibly not at all.

Once this realization takes hold, selling becomes irreversible in ways most assets never are.

That changes behavior permanently.

Why Re-Entry Risk Changes Everything

Most trading strategies assume re-entry is possible.

Sell now. Buy back later. Increase position size.

That logic works only when supply reliably returns to the market.

Bitcoin increasingly violates that assumption.

As supply becomes structurally unavailable, selling becomes a one-way door.

The question stops being:

> "Is this a good price to sell?"

It becomes:

> "Will I ever get this back?"

Credit Replaces Exit

When selling stops making sense, liquidity must come from somewhere else.

That source is credit.

Instead of selling Bitcoin, holders increasingly:

- Borrow against it
- Roll loans forward
- Refinance rather than liquidate
- Preserve ownership across cycles

This is not speculative leverage.

It is balance-sheet behavior.

Bitcoin shifts from something you trade to something you structure around.

Why This Is Not a Bubble Dynamic

Bubbles require eager sellers at higher prices.

- They require profit-taking.
- They require re-entry confidence.
- They require redistribution.

Bitcoin's structure now suppresses all three.

As selling declines, price must do more work to locate supply.

This produces moves that feel sudden, discontinuous, and unreasonable to those using old models.

But nothing is breaking.

The market is discovering that supply is gone.

Clearance Pricing Revisited

Earlier chapters introduced the idea of the clearance price.

This is not a top.
It is not a frenzy.

It is the price required to convince a holder to surrender something they believe cannot be replaced.

Clearance pricing is not emotional.

It is mechanical.

When selling stops making sense, price becomes the only remaining variable.

Time Preference Flips

Fiat systems reward spending and penalize saving. Bitcoin reverses that.

When holders expect appreciation driven by scarcity rather than productivity or growth, time preference flips.

Saving becomes rational.
Spending becomes optional.
Borrowing becomes strategic.

This shift is subtle but profound.

It changes how individuals plan, how institutions allocate, and how states think about reserves.

Why This Is a Repricing Event

Bull markets imply excess. Repricing implies correction.

Bitcoin's current phase is not excess demand. It is insufficient supply. The market is not discovering Bitcoin. It is discovering how little of it is available.

This is not a cycle peak. It is a structural adjustment.

Why This Can't Be Repeated

Every prior phase of Bitcoin allowed redistribution.

- Early adopters sold.
- New entrants bought.
- Supply recycled.

This phase does not.

Once Bitcoin enters permanent hands—collateralized, custodied, sovereign—it does not come back.

- There is no reset mechanism.
- There is no future "early phase."
- There is only positioning.

The Quiet End of the Old Question

For years, the central Bitcoin question was: "Is this the right time to buy?"

That question is fading.

The new question is simpler—and harder: "Will I ever be able to buy enough?"

Chapter 12 Summary

Selling Bitcoin is no longer a default behavior. It has become a strategic exception.

As supply migrates into permanent hands and credit replaces liquidation, markets lose their traditional clearing mechanism.

Price must rise until someone is willing to surrender what they believe they cannot replace.

That is not speculation.

That is structure asserting itself.

If selling is no longer the default release valve, the question
shifts.

Not *who buys next*, or *when price moves*, but **what happens to
a credit system when liquidation stops being the organizing
principle**.

Markets built on redistribution begin to behave differently when
assets are absorbed instead of recycled. Liquidity still enters, but
exits narrow. Risk is no longer expressed primarily through
price—it moves into structure.

The next chapter examines how modern credit systems respond
when faced with that reality: not through ideology or narrative,
but through balance sheets, collateral, and quiet re-anchoring.

Chapter 13—When Credit Systems Encounter the Reserve Layer

Drafted: December 2025

"In finance, stability is destabilizing."
— Hyman Minsky

This is not a theory or a prediction. It describes what happens when pressure becomes unavoidable and credit systems adapt accordingly.

Credit systems do not debate narratives. They adapt. Quietly, incrementally, and without announcements, they move toward whatever foundation best preserves value under stress.

This chapter describes that moment of recognition—when the mechanics of modern credit encounter absolute scarcity, and the system responds by re-anchoring itself.

Banks Respond to Balance-Sheet Reality

Banks don't follow stories. They respond to problems.

The financial system worked because the foundation seemed solid. Government bonds were trusted. Inflation felt contained. Credit could safely grow on top of that base.

That foundation is now under strain. What's changing isn't politics or technology—it's what banks can rely on when stress hits.

Banks care about balance sheets. They worry about how long assets are locked up, how easily they can be sold in a crisis, whether they quietly lose value over time, and whether they can be trusted when markets freeze.

When Traditional Reserve Assets Fail Together

Today, many traditional reserve assets share the same weaknesses:

- inflation slowly erodes them

- political decisions affect their value
- they tend to fail together in crises
- they are hard to audit quickly and clearly

These problems don't arrive all at once. They show up as pressure—tighter lending, higher capital requirements, and less room for mistakes. When that pressure builds, banks don't look for a new currency. They look for stronger collateral.

Bitcoin as Collateral, Not Currency

Bitcoin appears—not as spending money, not as a replacement for banks, and not as a trade.

Bitcoin shows up as a simple idea:

a scarce, global asset that doesn't depend on any institution and can be verified at any time.

Bitcoin doesn't replace credit.

It sits beneath it.

Loans are still made in dollars. Credit still expands. Fiat still circulates. What changes is the anchor under the system—the asset expected to hold value when everything else is stressed.

From this view, banks offering custody or lending against Bitcoin isn't belief or endorsement. It's practical. Assets that are easy to verify, hard to debase, and globally liquid tend to become collateral.

This isn't a philosophical shift.

It's a structural one.

In the past, gold played this role. But gold is slow, hard to move, and difficult to integrate into modern digital finance. Bitcoin fits the digital world. It settles quickly. It can be audited continuously. Its supply doesn't change.

Re-Anchoring Happens Quietly

Banks don't announce these transitions. They move gradually—first holding Bitcoin for clients, then lending against it, then quietly treating it as a foundational asset rather than something to trade.

By the time it's obvious, the shift is already underway.

Bitcoin isn't replacing banks. The system isn't being torn down. It's being re-anchored.

Credit still flows. Institutions remain. But the layer beneath them becomes harder.

And once that happens, selling Bitcoin no longer feels like moving into something better. It feels like giving up the foundation.

Not because Bitcoin wins, but because when absolute scarcity sits beneath global credit, there's nothing more solid to rotate into.

By now, a pattern should be clear.

Across holders, institutions, credit markets, and policy responses, Bitcoin is no longer behaving like an asset waiting for its next cycle. It is increasingly acting as a reference point—something other systems must adapt around, rather than reset against.

This shift does not require agreement.
It does not depend on belief.
And it does not arrive all at once.

It shows up through behavior.

Selling slows.
Holding periods lengthen.
Credit reorganizes.
Old assumptions stop working as expected.

What matters next is not a prediction about price, but a question of framework.

When a credit system shifts onto a new foundation, the change shows up in everyday behavior. What counts as acceptable collateral changes. People start holding assets longer. Selling happens less often—not because it's blocked, but because selling no longer helps people improve their position.

As that pattern settles in, prices stop acting like a release valve that clears the market. Instead, they start reflecting pressure that has been building quietly over time. The system no longer resets through waves of selling. It adjusts through prices moving higher.

This isn't another familiar cycle repeating. It's a change in conditions. And once that change takes hold, the market stops rotating the way it used to and enters a new phase shaped by limited supply.

The final chapter steps back from individual mechanisms and looks at the broader result of everything described so far: the emergence of a new Market Phase—defined less by repetition and more by constraint, less by narrative and more by structure.

By this point, conviction should not feel like optimism.

If it does, something has been misunderstood.

Structural conviction doesn't come from believing price will rise. It comes from understanding why selling becomes harder to justify with time. When the reasons for selling quietly disappear—when effort, cash, and promises no longer offer refuge across time—holding stops being a speculative act and becomes a rational one.

This is not bullishness in the emotional sense. It's alignment.
It's what happens when incentives, structure, and time stop
working against you.

At this point, only one objection remains—the claim that future
cryptography undermines everything described so far.

Quantum Computing and Cryptographic Migration

Quantum computing is often framed as a decisive threat to Bitcoin.
That framing obscures the actual issue.

The risk is neither imminent nor existential. It is specific, limited,
and already understood.

Modern digital systems—including Bitcoin—rely on a
cryptographic asymmetry: certain operations are easy to verify but
extremely difficult to reverse. In Bitcoin's case, this includes
private keys and digital signatures. A classical computer can verify
a signature almost instantly, while deriving the private key that
produced it would require infeasible amounts of time.

That asymmetry is what secures the system.

Quantum computers do not change this by being "faster"
computers. They change it by processing information differently.
For certain mathematical problems, a sufficiently capable quantum
machine could reduce the time required to solve them from
effectively impossible to theoretically feasible.

That is the concern.

But the scope matters.

Quantum computers do not threaten Bitcoin's ledger, its supply, or
its consensus mechanism. They do not rewrite the blockchain, alter
proof-of-work, forge blocks, or reverse final settlement. The
protocol itself is not exposed.

The only credible risk is key exposure.

Specifically: if a Bitcoin address reveals its public key and leaves funds unmoved for an extended period, a future quantum system—at sufficient scale—could theoretically derive the corresponding private key.

That risk applies narrowly:

- to address reuse
- to older or poorly managed wallet practices
- not to funds that are secured and moved using modern standards

Bitcoin does not require public keys to be exposed until funds are spent. In current wallet designs, keys remain hidden until use and can be rotated immediately afterward. The system already limits its attack surface by default.

The situation is best understood as a migration problem, not a failure mode.

A useful parallel is Y2K. In the 1990s, software systems stored years using two digits, creating a known rollover risk. The issue was real, the timeline was long, and the solution was adaptation. Engineers identified the constraint early and upgraded systems quietly before it mattered.

Nothing broke—not because the risk was imaginary, but because it was addressed in advance.

Quantum computing presents a similar profile:

- the vulnerability is known
- the exposure is specific
- the timeline is long
- the mitigation path is clear

Cryptography evolves. Bitcoin is not a static system. It has already undergone multiple cryptographic and protocol upgrades without breaking continuity or trust. Migration to quantum-resistant signature schemes would follow the same pattern: new address types, gradual adoption, and voluntary movement of funds over time.

No rewrite of history.
No reset of supply.
No fork of value.

Just evolution.

Funds held in modern wallets, moved periodically, or secured through updated standards would remain protected. Long-term holders would adapt the way they always have—deliberately, transparently, and well before urgency appears.

Quantum computing does not automatically invalidate the structural argument of this book, but it is a real constraint worth tracking. If quantum capability advances faster than mitigation and coordination, it becomes a meaningful risk to the framework's assumptions about custody and credit.

Systems that endure are not those that deny future constraints, but those designed to adapt to them without central coordination.

Bitcoin's durability will depend on timely upgrades and broad operational discipline—exactly the kind of constraint that makes this framework testable.

The Alignment

By the time scarcity becomes obvious, the outcome is already constrained. What's left isn't persuasion—it's permission.

Bitcoin reprices when sellable supply is scarce and marginal liquidity stops demanding forced sellers.

The firewood has been stacking for years. Not the idea of scarcity, but the reality of it. Bitcoin held with no intention of sale. Bitcoin used as collateral instead of being liquidated. Bitcoin absorbed into long-term holdings, custody, and balance sheets. This supply isn't waiting for a higher price. It's simply not for sale.

At that point, the pieces of the move are already in place:

Firewood: a lack of liquid supply—Bitcoin that isn't available at any reasonable price.
Kindling: fragile positioning—expiring shorts, aging leverage, trades that only work while pressure stays high.
The Match: alignment—the moment selling stops being necessary.
Ignition: liquidity—not as a cause, but as the removal of friction.
Wind: macro conditions—affecting speed and intensity, not direction.
Flame: repricing—driven by missing sellers, not sudden excitement.

Fragile positioning surrounds that firewood. Shorts that require constant rollover. Leverage that decays with time. Structures that hold together only while funding is tight and volatility is low. None of this creates the move, but it makes the system sensitive to release.

Alignment is when that release happens.

It doesn't require a dramatic event. It occurs when liquidity eases just enough that capital no longer needs Bitcoin to be sold. Funding pressure relaxes. Access improves. Optionality returns. The system finally has room to breathe.

Liquidity lights the fire not because it explains Bitcoin, but because it removes friction. In a market already short supply and long fragility, even modest liquidity can be enough to expose constraint. Shorts stop rolling cleanly. Sellers thin out. In that regime, price can move less on enthusiasm and more on missing supply.

Macro doesn't cause this shift. Macro is the wind. It can slow things down, speed them up, or shake the market along the way. But it can't create scarcity, and it can't start the fire on its own.

When liquidity meets alignment in a market already stripped of sellable supply, repricing doesn't creep higher. It snaps.

This is the point where the thesis stops being theoretical.

The alignment isn't the conclusion of the argument.
It's the moment the argument begins to function.

Once selling stops being necessary, the system doesn't reset on a clock. It adjusts to constraint. Collateral replaces liquidation. Holding periods extend. Scarcity compounds.

How Sovereigns Actually Accumulate

Most people assume sovereign states acquire scarce assets directly.

Historically, they do not.

When an asset is finite, globally traded, politically sensitive, and highly price-reactive, open accumulation works against the buyer. Purchasing at scale in public markets simply raises the price before the position is complete.

As a result, states tend to rely on indirect pathways; commercial intermediaries, state-linked institutions, and market participants with aligned incentives.

Not to hide activity—but to avoid moving the market against themselves.

This approach is not unusual. It is how reserves, commodities, and strategic resources have been accumulated for decades. The objective is not secrecy. It is price discipline.

Large buyers do not seek attention.
They seek time.

Which is why accumulation phases often appear unremarkable. Price moves sideways. Narratives fade. Activity looks fragmented or indecisive.

Until it isn't.

By the time accumulation becomes obvious, the window has already closed.

What follows is not a return to familiar rhythms, but a different operating condition—one where price no longer clears markets through excess, but pressures them through absence.

The final chapter steps back from the mechanics and looks at what this shift means once it is underway—and why, after alignment, the system does not easily go back.

Chapter 14—The New Bitcoin Market Phase

Drafted: December 2025

"Every system eventually reveals what it was really built to do."
— Author Unknown

Bitcoin was interpreted through a familiar framework. Markets assumed cycles would repeat, supply would redistribute, fiat would remain the unquestioned anchor, and credit would continue expanding without hard limits.

That framework no longer describes reality.

Bitcoin has crossed a threshold. What replaces the old model is not collapse or revolution, but a new Market Phase—defined by how participants actually behave, not how they are expected to behave.

The Defining Characteristics of the New Market Phase

The new Bitcoin Market Phase is shaped by five irreversible shifts:

- Circulating supply does not freely return
- Selling is replaced by collateralization
- Cycles give way to repricing
- Fiat is demoted, not destroyed
- Bitcoin becomes generational collateral

These shifts describe current directional behavior, not permanence. If circulating supply begins returning at scale— through sustained liquidation, policy reversal, or prolonged credit contraction—the pattern weakens visibly.

The framework is conditional on duration continuing to outweigh distribution.

These are not ideological claims.

They are observable behavioral outcomes already in motion.

Bitcoin as Stored Generational Wealth

Bitcoin is not money in motion.

It is stored generational wealth—an asset optimized not for spending but for preserving purchasing power across time, political systems, Market Phases, and monetary failures.

This is why Bitcoin does not function as the world's everyday currency.

Currencies must circulate.
Bitcoin must not.

Its resistance to circulation is not a flaw.

It is the source of its power.

Why Bitcoin Becomes Collateral First

Bitcoin naturally evolves into collateral for one simple reason: it appreciates structurally over long-time horizons.

Not because price moves straight up, but because circulating supply contracts while global demand for neutral, incorruptible collateral expands.

As long as ownership is retained:

- the base asset is never consumed

- collateral value renews itself over time
- borrowing capacity can be rolled forward

Spending ends utility. Collateralization extends it.

Collateralization is reinforced not only by holder preference, but by institutional structures that continue operating through volatility—regulated ETF vehicles, treasury allocation mandates, custody infrastructure, and balance-sheet accounting treatment.

These systems function on policy and duration, not trading reflex. If those structures weaken or reverse, collateral dominance weakens with them.

This logic holds at every level—individual, institutional, and sovereign.

What Happens When Fiat Fails as a Store of Value

Fiat does not disappear. It is demoted.

When fiat fails as a store of value, it still functions as a medium of exchange, a unit of account, and a tax and spending rail. What it loses is its role as a savings anchor.

Bitcoin absorbs that role.

The system shifts from:

saving in fiat and borrowing in fiat

to:

saving in Bitcoin and borrowing in fiat

Credit does not vanish.

It re-anchors.

Why the System No Longer Resets

Previous Bitcoin cycles reset through forced selling, capitulation, and redistribution.

Those mechanisms are fading.

Permanent holders do not sell.
Institutions rebalance less frequently.
Sovereigns do not trade reserves.

Without forced liquidation, the classic winter season loses its mechanisms.

There are pauses and consolidations—but not resets.

When Capital Markets Reorganize Around Bitcoin

Once Bitcoin is treated as permanent collateral, traditional financial instruments begin to behave differently.

What firms like Strategy demonstrated was not financial innovation, but financial reorganization:

- Equity becomes a volatility wrapper around Bitcoin
- convertible debt monetizes optionality without liquidation
- straight debt is underwritten by appreciating collateral
- structured claims stack risk profiles above the same BTC base

Time stops being the enemy.

Finance does not invent new tools.

It rearranges existing ones around a balance sheet that does not empty.

Bitcoin-backed Lending Institutions

Alongside Bitcoin-native capital markets, a parallel system of Bitcoin-backed lending has emerged.

These institutions allow individuals, families, and organizations to access liquidity by borrowing against Bitcoin instead of selling it. While still early, this ecosystem is already global and expanding.

Bitcoin-backed lending is not a niche experiment.

It is a structural response to a world in which selling Bitcoin becomes increasingly inefficient.

As this reality becomes clearer, traditional banks, private credit providers, and sovereign-adjacent institutions will enter through acquisition, partnership, or internal build-out.

The identity of the lender matters less than the model:

- Bitcoin is permanent collateral, not inventory
- liquidity is accessed without liquidation
- loans are rolled, resized, or refinanced
- fiat becomes a spending rail, not savings

This is not banking being disrupted.

It is banking adapting.

What This Means—Depending on Who You Are

For economists:

Mean reversion breaks. Bitcoin introduces an external, appreciating collateral that constrains monetary discretion without coordination.

For technologists:

Bitcoin is not competing with applications. It is the settlement layer they reference. Its power comes from refusal to change.

For sovereign states:

Bitcoin does not replace sovereignty. It disciplines it. States that move early gain balance-sheet credibility before announcements are ever made.

For institutions:

Bitcoin is no longer an alternative asset. It becomes the benchmark. The risk shifts from volatility to under-exposure.

For families and savers:

Bitcoin is not about getting rich. It is about ensuring today's work still matters tomorrow—and for the next generation. You don't trade it. You hold it. If needed, you borrow against it.

Why Bitcoin Cannot Be Recreated

Bitcoin persists not through innovation, but through finality. Its rules are fixed. Its governance is absent. Its monetary policy is untouchable.

Any attempt to improve it would destroy the very property that makes it credible.

Bitcoin is not the best technology.

It is the last credible monetary constant.

This Is the New Market Phase

In this Market Phase:

- price discovery is discontinuous
- volatility clusters upward
- collateral matters more than yield
- credibility matters more than growth
- time favors holders, not traders

Bitcoin does not run the system. It anchors it.

Limits of the Framework

This framework describes how Bitcoin behaves *if* certain structural conditions persist.

It rests on observable mechanisms, not guarantees.

The thesis weakens under three specific conditions:

1. Sellable supply meaningfully returns
If Bitcoin held as long-duration collateral, institutional reserves, or sovereign balance-sheet assets begins to re-enter the market at scale, the constraint described throughout this book loosens. That would restore redistribution, revive traditional clearing behavior, and reintroduce cycle dynamics that depend on willing sellers at higher prices.

2. Forced liquidation overwhelms credit substitution
If regulatory action, systemic failure, or legal compulsion forces widespread liquidation of Bitcoin holdings—beyond the capacity of credit markets to absorb—then selling once again becomes the

dominant release mechanism.
In that scenario, the transition from liquidation to collateralization
stalls or reverses.

3. A credible alternative emerges with superior properties
This framework assumes no other system simultaneously matches
Bitcoin's monetary scarcity, neutrality, settlement finality,
auditability, and resistance to control—while also improving
liquidity at scale.
Such an alternative is not impossible. It is simply unobserved.

None of these conditions are theoretical. All are measurable.

This is not a claim that the system cannot change. It is a claim that
change leaves evidence.

If sellable supply expands, the framework fails.
If forced selling dominates, the framework fails.
If superior monetary infrastructure replaces Bitcoin's role, the
framework fails.

Until then, the behavior described here is not speculative.
It is structural.

This framework fails if:

- Exchange balances expand persistently
- Long-term holder supply contracts materially
- Bitcoin-backed credit contracts instead of expands
- Sovereign and institutional participation reverses

These conditions are observable.

If they occur, the structural compression thesis weakens or fails.

Final Orientation

This book does not ask for belief.
It documents a structural shift already visible in market
behavior.

Bitcoin's role has changed not because narratives improved or
adoption accelerated, but because the conditions that once
forced it to circulate have weakened. Selling is no longer
required to access liquidity. Supply no longer returns reliably at
higher prices. Credit increasingly substitutes for liquidation.

Those changes alter how markets clear.

When assets circulate freely, markets reset through selling.
When circulation tightens, markets adjust through price.

What has emerged is not a new story about Bitcoin, but a
different operating condition. Ownership has shifted toward
balance sheets. Holding periods have lengthened. Sellable
supply has thinned. Price has become resistant not because
demand is euphoric, but because exits no longer scale.

At that point, Bitcoin stops behaving like an asset waiting for its
next cycle and begins functioning as a reference—something
other systems increasingly adapt around rather than reset
against.

This framework does not rely on inevitability. It relies on
mechanics.

It would fail only if sellable supply returned meaningfully at
scale.
It would fail if holders were structurally forced to liquidate
rather than refinance.
It would fail if an alternative system emerged that matched

Bitcoin's scarcity, neutrality, verifiability, and settlement finality while materially improving on them.

These conditions are observable. They are not currently implied by the behavior described here.

Markets do not announce transitions. They reveal them through what stops working.

When selling no longer improves position, holding ceases to be speculative.
When liquidation gives way to collateral, cycles lose their force.
When supply tightens quietly, price becomes the remaining adjustment.

This is not a prediction about what Bitcoin will become—it describes how markets behave when selling stops making sense.

Continue the Work

If the ideas in this book resonate with you, the next step is to apply the framework in real market conditions.

The **Reading Bitcoin Structured Framing Session** is a guided working program designed to help participants develop a disciplined method for interpreting Bitcoin through Market State.

Participants work directly with the framework introduced in this book — using consistent dashboards, structured prompts, and an LLM analytical partner — to learn how to generate their own Market State reports on demand.

The goal is not prediction.
The goal is orientation.

More information is available at:

BTCintelligence.ai